Gathering My Stones

A devotional book of poetry

© 2010

By Janet A. Brooks

MARTON
PUBLISHING INTL
Words for the World

This book is dedicated to

My Lord and Savior, Jesus Christ, who is the author and giver of all good things!

My mother, who has believed in me and encouraged me to get these printed for many years.

All of my family for their overwhelming support and love through the years, in season and out!

Contents

PREFACE

Jacob was on a journey, a journey that would lead him into the arms of a powerful God and all the adventures that God had ordained for him.

At the insistence of his over-adoring mother, Jacob was fleeing his brother's wrath. Jacob had just stolen his brother's birthright, not a great condition to be in when God came to visit. He was headed away from family, friends and all that was familiar.

On that first night away from home, lonely, probably homesick and afraid, he placed a stone under his head and tried to sleep. In a dream, God showed him the blessings that would be given him, the best of which was His very Presence. God said to the quivering Jacob, "I will be with you and keep you wherever you go."

Jacob awoke from his dream and said, "Surely the Lord is in this place and I did not know it." Then he feared God and worshipped Him. "This place where I am now, under the stars, with a stone as my pillow, is none other than the house of God. How awesome is this place. God is here!"

So Jacob took the stone upon which he laid his dream-filled head and set it up as a pillar, a sign, "GOD HAS BEEN HERE." He poured oil upon it to say, "This is a holy place, a sacred place, for I have met God here." The pillar was a sign of covenant between Jacob and God.

But still, Jacob had much to learn about God. He tried to make a bargain with God: "If God will go with me, then He will be my God." God had already promised to be with him but Jacob had yet to learn that God always keeps His promises.

My life has been a journey, too, a journey of following a God I am more and more in love with every day, as He continues to lead. He has met me at every curve; He has sustained me in every valley; He has lifted me up to the heights and revealed Himself to me as much as I can stand.

I have gathered my stones, my signs of covenant, at the place of our meetings. Every encounter has been one of revelation: about Himself, about me, about the world. In every emotional twist and turn of my journey, He has been faithful. He has always kept His promises, even when I doubted Him.

These stones I have gathered are really gifts created and given to me by God. My heart received them, my pen wrote the words but my Father inspired them. To Him be the glory forever and ever.

I pray that these gifts will stir in your heart a hope, a thought, a longing for more.

GATHERING MY STONES

Bring some comfort to my soul, my Lord
It seems our afflictions
Have followed us for so many years
Like stones along the creek bank
They lay
Not dissolving or floating away
But as the water of the Holy Spirit
Washes through the rivers of our lives
Those stones of suffering
Become gems whose beauty are beyond measure
Gems of faithfulness, endurance
Deliverance, patience, intercession
Delivered by the very hand of God

The pure life-giving water
Softens the jagged edges
And we can see your face reflected in each trial
Your hand upon each life
Your grace covering all

I will rest by that stream, Lord
I do not have to make myself a bed
In pastures green
But beside the still waters
I will lay my head
On the stones You have fashioned for me

Praise

Our God inhabits praise. As we praise Him, He changes us. I used to think praise was for when you feel good already, have all the answers already, and are rejoicing in your close relationship to God. I thought praise was all those warm and fuzzy feelings, welling up and bubbling over before His throne.

But I have learned somewhere along the way that praise is the most important part of the spiritual battles we are called to fight. No matter how I feel, or what questions I have, or what terrible circumstance I am in or how much I have failed in my Christian walk, praising Him will carry me to a different place.

When I praise Him, He changes me. My complaints become thanksgiving; my sorrows grow small; the battle is won in my heart and I can see His hand during my day.

YOUR CREATION SPEAKS

Your creation shouts of Your glory
The sunshine screams Your majesty
Even the fog subtly covers us
With the blanket of Your love
The cool breeze touches my cheek
The smell of Fall on Your breath

And when You speak to me
My heart beats faster
My soul runs through Your fields
All green now, soon to be covered with snow
Every season showing Your creation
Your mind, Your glory
How can anyone not believe in You?

Since what may be known about God is plain to them, because God has made it plain to them. For since the creation of the world God's invisible qualities—his eternal power and divine nature—have been clearly seen, being understood from what has been made, so that men are without excuse. (Romans 1:19-20)

GLORY TO OUR KING

Sing the song of the angels
Glory, glory, glory to our King
The glow of the coming sun
Wraps the earth in angel halo
Glory, glory, glory to our King
Frosty whiteness lies on the ground
Anticipation of blankets of purity
Glory, glory, glory to our King

Praise be to the LORD God, the God of Israel, who alone does marvelous deeds. Praise be to his glorious name forever; may the whole earth be filled with his glory. Amen and Amen. (Psalm 72:18-19)

IN DIFFERENT WAYS

Praises rush from the lips
Of one whose arms are held high
Dancing with the joy of You
Being overcome by emotions too strong
For human language
Every strain of the melody lively
Seen in eyes and hands
And body and feet
No inhibitions, no requirements
Nothing left unseen
To those who join
As visitors

Poised and staid
While organ strains
Pour out the beautiful music
Of those long past
Who have used their gifts for You
Hands folded and heads bowed
In Holy reverence
Nothing to indicate the depth of worship
Coming from deep within
Except one tear
No words to express

The well of emotions, which lies quietly
Behind the veil
Where the encounter is happening
A meeting with the Holy One
One cannot judge worship by the length of the song
Nor the movement of the body
Only the heart
May my heart be found
In the position of praise
No matter where I go to worship

So what shall I do? I will pray with my spirit, but I will also pray with my mind; I will sing with my spirit, but I will also sing with my mind. (1 Corinthians 14:15)

GOD OF ALL

Praise to You, God
The God of the rough and unrefined
The God of the changed drug-addict
The recovering alcoholic
The raspy-voiced chain smoker

Praise and glory to You, Jesus
The God of the refined,
The beautiful, the healthy
The polite and sweet

You are the God of all of me
Because I am all those things
Don't ever let me be fooled
By my education or flowing words
Or talents or wisdom
We all stand naked before You
Praise to You, God
Who sees us as we are
And still loves us
"I glory in Your grace"

Therefore, since we have been justified through faith, we have peace with God through our Lord Jesus Christ, through whom we have gained access by faith into this grace in which we now stand. And we rejoice in the hope of the glory of God. (Romans 5:1-2)

TO CREATE A GOD

If we were to create a god
In our own image
Would he hold the power of the universe
In his hand?
Would his love cover the expanse of the skies
And overflow the depth of the ocean?
Would his compassion
Bring forgiveness for multitudes of sins
Committed by those who don't even acknowledge his
name?
Would he treat his children with such loving discipline?
Would he care so much that they be holy?

If we were to create a god in our own image
Would he know the beginning to the end?
Would he hold eternity in his heart?
Would his patience be unlimited?
His thoughts above our thoughts?
His ways above our ways?
Would his glory fill the earth
And light the heavens?
Would myriads of angels sing at his feet?
And call out "Worthy is the Lamb
To receive power and glory and honor"

Then Job replied to the LORD: "I know that you can do all things; no plan of yours can be thwarted. You asked, 'Who is this that obscures my counsel without knowledge?' Surely I spoke of things I did not understand, things too wonderful for me to know. "You said, 'Listen now, and I will speak; I will question you, and you shall answer me.' (Job answers) My ears had heard of you but now my eyes have seen you. (Job 42:1-5)

PRAISING AS I AM

I wish I had more to give You, Lord
Than this broken down heap of tired flesh
Dragging from one task to the next
With all my heart, the depths of every pain
I give my praise to You
I worship You, I love You
With all my mind
Which seems to flicker on and off
As though some connection has worn out

I worship You, I love You
With all my strength
Such as it is (or isn't!)
I worship You. I love You
Restore my heart, O God
To love You more
Heal every wound
Give me a transfusion this morning, Lord
Bring rest to my mind
Sharpen it, bring connection back
So that I can hear Your plans
That I can write them down clearly

Renew my strength like the eagle
That I may not grow weary
In my walking and my running
I wait upon You, Lord
Such as I am
I worship You
And You tell me,
That is enough

O Lord, open my lips, and my mouth will declare your praise. You do not delight in sacrifice, or I would bring it; you do not take pleasure in burnt offerings. The sacrifices of God are a broken spirit; a broken and contrite heart, O God, you will not despise. (Psalm 51:15-17)

PSALM 18

You, oh Lord, have set me in a wide place
When I thought my emotions would strangle me
All energy, creativity, confidence
Seeping from me
Pouring out from beneath the deadly grip
Of depression and burn-out
You, Oh my God, reached down
And picked me up
You set me free to once again praise Your name
How awesome are Your works, O Lord
In my life
With You, I can leap over walls
Without You, I am lost

He brought me out into a spacious place; he rescued me because he delighted in me. You save the humble but bring low those whose eyes are haughty. You, O LORD, keep my lamp burning; my God turns my darkness into light. With your help I can advance against a troop; with my God I can scale a wall. (Psalm 18:19, 27-29)

BE EXALTED

Let Your name be exalted in all the earth
Oh Christ, Victor triumphant
From the ends of the earth
May Your songs ripple across the waters
Your glory riding on the crests of the waves
May stories of Your miracles
Surround the globe

*Like your name, O God, your praise reaches to the ends
of the earth; your right hand is filled with righteousness.
(Psalm 48:10)*

BEYOND UNDERSTANDING

I cannot fathom the depths of You, Jehovah
The expanse, the glory
The eternity of Your power
The mysterious working of Your Spirit

Reveal Yourself to me, O God
That I might know You
Strengthen me so that I will be able to
Hold the fullness of You

*'For my thoughts are not your thoughts, neither are your
ways my ways,' declares the LORD. (Isaiah 55:8)*

GLORIOUS FATHER

Glorious Father
In You is the light of the sun
The brilliance of the stars
Let Your light shine upon me, oh God
That I, like the moon
Might be a reflection of Your glory

You are the light of the world. A city on a hill cannot be hidden. (Matthew 5:14)

THE DANCE

I sometimes dance around
In circles
One foot in front of the other
Arms flailing overhead
The cloud of dirt rises
To cover my face
With each stomp I cry
"Why? Why? Why?"
The particles fill my nose
My throat; sting my eyes
Until I can no longer see or speak

I sometimes dance around
My soul feet making
Beautiful patterns
Not of my own design
Arms outstretched in grace
And praise
With each move I make
I sing
"I love you! I love you! I love you!"

Your glory fills my being
And I am lifted far above
Any thought, or desire or feeling
That I have ever known

Take all my dances, Lord
I am Your child
Forgive my childishness
I love the way You
Take my flailing arms
And stomping feet
And ever so gently
Break them
And begin to make them into
Praising arms, glory feet
Oh, that all of me
At all times, in all situations
Would dance only for Your glory

David, wearing a linen ephod, danced before the LORD with all his might, while he and the entire house of Israel brought up the ark of the LORD with shouts and the sound of trumpets. (2 Samuel 6:14)

MY FATHER'S WORLD

Life, whether in the heavenlies or here on earth
Is worth the living
Living in His Presence
Always
Seeing the beauty in the sunrise
The budding flower
The falling snow
The laugh of a baby
Kisses between a long married couple
Absorbing the warmth of the suns rays
Feeling refreshed by the cool wind
The touch of a hand on my face
Or a pat on my back

Listening to the music of those filled by Your Spirit
Inspired by Your heart
Orchestra and band
Country quartet and unaccompanied shower soloist
Hearing the songs of the birds after a rainy night
Sounds translated into love messages
From You

Your world, this world
Is full of You
Your hand touches the skies
The mountains shout Your name
Your children laugh and cry and get angry
But we love You and each other
Together we stand in Your power
Against the evil that threatens
To take away all that is so lovely
In Your world
Clinging to the beauty we have in You

This IS my Father's world
For the beauty of this world
I will raise my hands to You in ceaseless praise
Until the time You choose
To take me home!!

God saw all that he had made, and it was very good. And there was evening, and there was morning—the sixth day. (Genesis 1:31)

BEAUTY

(Written on the last day of a stay at a B&B in Amish country before going back to our work in the inner city)

You take my breath away, Creator God
From the songs of the plethora of birds
To the rolling hills on which horses graze
From this place on top of the mountain
We see Your hand, Your heart
Your mind is beautiful, O Lord
All the thoughts You have of us

Put this beauty in my heart Lord
Your hand, Your mind
Let me take it back
To places that aren't so beautiful
Let me hold Your grace on my tongue
Your song in my heart
Your beauty in my eyes

"Therefore I tell you, do not worry about your life, what you will eat or drink; or about your body, what you will wear. Is not life more important than food, and the body more important than clothes? Look at the birds of the air; they do not sow or reap or store away in barns, and yet your heavenly Father feeds them. Are you not much more valuable than they? (Matthew 6:25-26)

PRAISE PREPARATION

I lay basking in Your Presence
As in the Hawaiian sun
You ARE the sunshine in my life
There is nothing pressing on my heart
Just to praise You
And enjoy Your Presence

Thank You for this gift
Perhaps the calm before the storm?
The lull before the battle?
Where the heart rests and is prepared
My cry, O Lord, is always:
Use me to bring someone into Your Kingdom
I AM a missionary after all

*Let my teaching fall like rain and my words descend like
dew, like showers on new grass, like abundant rain on
tender plants. I will proclaim the name of the LORD. Oh,
praise the greatness of our God! He is the Rock, his works
are perfect, and all his ways are just. A faithful God who
does no wrong, upright and just is he.*
(Deuteronomy 32:2-4)

Jesus

There is never an end to knowing more of Jesus. I grew up knowing that He was my best friend. I innocently accepted the song of my preschool teachers, "My best friend is Jesus". I believed in Him as my Savior at nine. I fell in love with Him when I was thirteen. But I am still learning who He is and the depth of the meaning behind what He has done for me. The words of the old chorus are so true: "The longer I serve Him, the sweeter He grows."

"Now we see through a glass, darkly but someday we will see Him face to face and know Him." Oh what a glorious day that will be!

CHRISTMAS

Soft as the snow upon the ground
As the warm sunshine hastening
Through the window
To light up the colors of
Christmas
Jesus comes into our lives
Softly, warmly
Full of love and light
Brightening the colors of our lives
Putting Christmas in our hearts

In the beginning was the Word, and the Word was with God, and the Word was God. He was with God in the beginning. Through him all things were made; without him nothing was made that has been made. (John 1:1-3)

STAR

Star shining bright in the night sky
Bringing comfort after earthquakes
Speaking encouragement after fires
Constantly guiding during times of uncertainty
Showing peace to me
The clouds come and cover you
But I know you are there

The clouds are dispersed
As though pushed away
By a mighty hand
and again
You shine bright upon my world
Jesus, My Bright Morning Star

*And we have the word of the prophets made more
certain, and you will do well to pay attention to it, as to a
light shining in a dark place, until the day dawns and the
morning star rises in your hearts. (2 Peter 1:19)*

GIFTS FOR THE CHRIST CHILD

Sweet baby, lying in the manger
Purity, innocence
Royalty, divinity
Incarnate love
On the hard ground
The scholars kneel
Those who supposedly know all
Bowing to the One who
Knows all

What did the wise men see
As they laid their gifts beneath Your makeshift crib?
Little eyes, what depth of joy and sorrow
You would know

Little hands
Pierced through with nails
On behalf of all

Little heart
That beats with a love
That would take it to Calvary
Broken by sins that are not its own

Gifts we lay
Beneath Your humble throne
Gold for our King
Frankincense for our God
Myrrh for our Savior
O Come let us adore Him

On coming to the house, they saw the child with his mother Mary, and they bowed down and worshiped him. Then they opened their treasures and presented him with gifts of gold and of incense and of myrrh. (Matthew 2:11)

CHRISTMAS CANDLES

The plastic is stained from years of use
Or rather, the lack of it
Dirt in the cracks
Age spots appearing
In all the wrong places
Resurrected from the attic Christmas box
Where they sat in a tangled mess
For how many years
No one knows

Here they stand
Sedately doing what they were made to do
Cords aligned and plugged up
Their light brings a smile to my eyes
Remembering a time when
There was some debate
Over trashing them
Or not
Funny thing is…
The light is so bright
No one would notice
The flawed vessel
Through which it surges

Thank you Jesus
For being the Light of my Life

But we have this treasure in jars of clay to show that this all-surpassing power is from God and not from us. (2 Corinthians 4:7)

CHRISTMAS PEACE

Calmness fell upon the ragged shack
Like the rays of light
From the star above it
Thousands of people in the city
Scurrying to find food
To see long lost acquaintances
To drink and be merry
(If they weren't complaining
Because of no place to park their camels)

But in the little stable
Outside the inn
There was
Peace
The Lord of Peace was born
There was
Deep Joy
The Giver of Joy had come

Let the calmness of your arrival
Prevail in my heart, sweet Jesus
May peace and joy
Have the victory

As You make Your home
In every room of my heart

My heart is indeed on fire
With the light of Christmas

While they were there, the time came for the baby to be born, and she gave birth to her firstborn, a son. She wrapped him in cloths and placed him in a manger, because there was no room for them in the inn. (Luke 2:6-7)

SERVANT

He kneels before the friends
Who would deny Him
Betray Him

The sacred hands
That would be pierced
For that very denial

Take the rag
An ordinary rag
Not gold-trimmed or fine
But soon to be filthy
And dip it in the water
Clear, clean
Reviving

On the feet that will carry
His gospel to the ends of the earth
The Son of Man places His touch
Cleansing, healing
His white robe becomes brown
As His knees scrape across the dirt floor
His hands, once white and beautiful

Become dark with the grime
Of the everyday
As the feet of His disciples
Turn white and new

The servant portrays
A much deeper price
That soon will be paid
Not only for His disciples
But for all of mankind

It was just before the Passover Feast. Jesus knew that the time had come for him to leave this world and go to the Father. Having loved his own who were in the world, he now showed them the full extent of his love. (John 13:1)

THE CROSS

My human eyes look and see
Wood
Old, rugged
Splintered, hard and weathered
Rusty nails with stains of blood
My human heart sees pain
And cries," No Way"
There's no beauty in that instrument of death

But my spirit's eyes
See Jesus
The love in His eyes as He hangs there
The cleansing in His blood
As it pours from His body
My soul has seen its salvation
And the cross is transformed
Into glory
Bright, shining, pure gold
My suffering is changed into
Shouts of praise
And I gladly take my place
Beneath the cross!

For the message of the cross is foolishness to those who are perishing, but to us who are being saved it is the power of God. (1 Corinthians 1:18)

THE PASSION

(Written after seeing the movie The Passion of Christ)

An encounter that defies words
Soul-wrenching agony
As I watch my Savior
Beaten for my transgressions
The determination in His face
The torture spread across His brow
By His stripes, I am healed
And my soul cries out
"Thank you Jesus, Thank you, Jesus, Thank you, Jesus"

Holiness nailed to the cross
Perfection marred past knowing
A stumbling block to those who refuse to see
The path to victory for those who are hungry
VICTORY, as He stomped the serpents head
"Be gone, You tempter of the Son of God"
VICTORY, as He looked at His Mother
And said," Mother, I'm making all things new"
VICTORY spread across the screen
For all the nations to see
"I am the way, the truth, the life
No one comes to the Father but by me"

VICTORY in His resurrection smile
It is finished; accomplished; complete
Walking out of the tomb
In blinding glory
The world waits in anticipation
Enraptured by the One who did
What no man could do
"No man can take away the sins of the whole world"
But He did!
The great I AM!
"Thank you Jesus, Thank You Jesus, Thank You Jesus!"

He was despised and rejected by men, a man of sorrows, and familiar with suffering. Like one from whom men hide their faces he was despised, and we esteemed him not. Surely he took up our infirmities and carried our sorrows, yet we considered him stricken by God, smitten by him, and afflicted. But he was pierced for our transgressions, he was crushed for our iniquities; the punishment that brought us peace was upon him, and by his wounds we are healed. (Isaiah 53:3-5)

BEAUTY IN YOU

The filthy rags
Soiled and stained by years of neglect
And purposeful disdain
Made white as snow
No spot, no tear, no filth

Oh the beauty of the One
Who was and is and will ever be
Unspoiled, beautiful
The one who is pure
Who knows no sin
As He takes upon Himself
The filthy rags
He embraces them with all the pain
Of one who hates sin
More than He loves life
He takes the stain upon Himself
And finishes it---brings death to it
And all is made clean
White, pure, holy again
Oh, the beauty of Jesus

All of us have become like one who is unclean, and all our righteous acts are like filthy rags; we all shrivel up like a leaf, and like the wind our sins sweep us away. (Isaiah 64:6)

We all, like sheep, have gone astray, each of us has turned to his own way; and the LORD has laid on him the iniquity of us all. (Isaiah 53:6)

WHAT IS LOVE?

What is love?
I could say it's
The beauty of the flowers
Their vibrant and delicate colors
Yet they fade away and die

I could say
The vastness of the sky
The shades of blue touching my eyes
Like water drops to the soul
And yet, the sky turns dark and angry
The vastness closes in
And encompasses me with fear

I could say
The warmth of my family
Hugs and kisses, Christmas presents
And Thanksgiving dinners
Yet, in our humanity
Warmth can turn to coldness
Sharp words said from a hurting heart
Distance grows and special occasions
Become nothing but memories

I see Your love in the cross, Oh God
The emblem of suffering and shame
The symbol of Your sacrifice
On my account
The fact of my pardon
Not due to anything in me
Unchangeable, never invalidated
Always free
Never dependant
On time of year, or mood, or mind
The cross: real, steady, fact
Your crown of love for me
"So I cling to the old rugged cross
And exchange it some day for a crown"

When you were dead in your sins and in the uncircumcision of your sinful nature, God made you alive with Christ. He forgave us all our sins, having canceled the written code, with its regulations, that was against us and that stood opposed to us; he took it away, nailing it to the cross. And having disarmed the powers and authorities, he made a public spectacle of them, triumphing over them by the cross. (Colossians 2:13-15)

41

SUFFERING SERVANT

Lovely suffering servant
Was there always a tear behind Your smile?
A deep pool of painful compassion
Behind Your laugh?
Oh, how much You have to give
But people settle for crumbs
You desire to share
The secrets of the universe
And they seek for a good time

The burden is not an easy one
But with such deep love
You continue to hold out Your hand

"O Jerusalem, Jerusalem, you who kill the prophets and stone those sent to you, how often I have longed to gather your children together, as a hen gathers her chicks under her wings, but you were not willing. Look, your house is left to you desolate. (Matthew 23:37-38)

MY HIGH PRIEST

I am coming to my High Priest
My heart I bring as a sacrifice
A sweet fragrance
For the Holy One
Who sees me
Washed in the blood
And white as snow
How beautiful You are
In the sanctuary, my King
Your glory brighter than the sun
Your love surrounding, filling
Making me warm
No words to say, but heartfelt praise
For One who was and is and is yet to come

Therefore, since we have a great high priest who has gone through the heavens, Jesus the Son of God, let us hold firmly to the faith we profess. We have this hope as an anchor for the soul, firm and secure. It enters the inner sanctuary behind the curtain, where Jesus, who went before us, has entered on our behalf. He has become a high priest forever, in the order of Melchizedek.
(Hebrews 4:14, 6:19-20)

TO BE LIKE YOU

You who spoke the world into being
Who could outspeak any philosopher
You chose to grace your followers with stories
Of flowers and lost coins and family squabbles
The beauty of Your self-control
The depth of Your wisdom

To have the ability to bring down the government
But reaching down to a small child
To know that the rocks and hills cry out Your praise
But You endure the unbelief of those closest to You
To have the power to cast into heaven or hell
And You whisper, "Father, forgive them'

I want to be like You, Jesus
Limit my profundity of words
To those You choose
Let the notes I play
Be perfectly placed
Let my actions
Reflect the beauty of Your grace
The tenderness of Your smile
Let my prayers in front of others
Be simple

Who, being in very nature God, did not consider equality with God something to be grasped, but made himself nothing, taking the very nature of a servant, being made in human likeness. And being found in appearance as a man, he humbled himself and became obedient to death— even death on a cross! (Philippians 2:6-8)

LOVER OF MY SOUL

Jesus lover of my soul
You woo me to yourself
With fields of flowers
You display your love to me
In the majestic mountains
You sing of Your faithfulness
Through the birds chirping
Outside my window
What better lover
What better friend
Could I ask for?

My lover spoke and said to me, "Arise, my darling, my
beautiful one, and come with me. See! The winter is past;
the rains are over and gone. Flowers appear on the earth;
the season of singing has come, the cooing of doves is
heard in our land. The fig tree forms its early fruit; the
blossoming vines spread their fragrance. Arise, come, my
darling; my beautiful one, come with me."
Lover: My dove in the clefts of the rock, in the hiding
places on the mountainside, show me your face, let me
hear your voice; for your voice is sweet, and your face is
lovely. (Song of Solomon 2:10-14)

THE LIGHT

Walk in the light
As I am in the light
I AM the light of the world
Let me be the light in you
Warming you
Guiding your way
Illuminating your life
In such a way
That you do not stumble
Let the world be attracted to
My light in you
Be my light in the darkness

When Jesus spoke again to the people, he said, "I am the light of the world. Whoever follows me will never walk in darkness, but will have the light of life." (John 8:12)

VICTORY OVER DEATH

The rocks are shaken
The veil is split
The whole world trembles
By the power revealed
Through a wooden cross
And a rock tomb
Objects, at first,
Of contempt
Both, places of death
And suffering
But God, the all-powerful
Transformed them

The cross—a gateway to God
And the empty tomb—
A podium of victory
Praise to the transformer
Who takes what is nothing
And makes it something
Who takes what is contemptible
And makes it victorious

For the perishable must clothe itself with the imperishable, and the mortal with immortality. When the perishable has been clothed with the imperishable, and the mortal with immortality, then the saying that is written will come true: "Death has been swallowed up in victory." "Where, O death, is your victory? Where, O death, is your sting?" (I Corinthians 15:53-55)

○ ○ ◯ ○ ◌

JESUS

Human Jesus, servant Jesus
You fully submitted to Your Father's will
King with all rights
You willingly laid down Your life
In spite of feelings
In spite of followers
Telling You to go a different way
Beautiful picture of submission
Be ever before me
That I might be like You

He went away a second time and prayed, "My Father, if it is not possible for this cup to be taken away unless I drink it, may your will be done." (Matthew 26:42)

MAKE ME LIKE YOU

Gentle Jesus, King of all
Mighty warrior
Servant of sinners
You did not grasp what was rightfully yours
The power, the kingdom, the glory
You became insignificant
In the eyes of many
Choosing to reveal Yourself
Only to a few

You placed Your kingdom in the hearts of men
Where sometimes they recognized You as Lord
And sometimes not…
You make Yourself available to be chosen
Never forcing Your treasures on anyone
You lived the life of Your Father, servant King
With determination, joy, purpose
Oh, the example that You give to me
I want to be like You, Jesus

I have set you an example that you should do as I have done for you. (John 13:15)

MARANATHA

There is dancing
On the streets of gold
Exuberance filling the air
As old people dance jigs
And young ones turn somersaults
The King is preparing for battle
The angels blow the trumpets
Not yet loud enough
For those on earth to hear
A tuning up for the final battle call
White stallions dance with anticipation
Ready for the clouds to be rolled back
As the world ushers in
Her King of Kings
Lord of Lords
Maranatha
Come, Lord Jesus

He who testifies to these things says, "Yes, I am coming soon." (Maranatha) Amen. Come, Lord Jesus (Revelation 22:20)

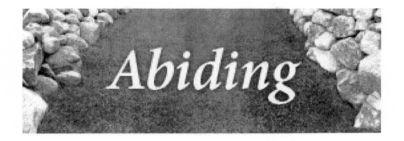

Abiding

When I think of abiding, I think of resting in a warm and cozy, safe place. I think of peace and joy. It is that place where, no matter what is happening around me or to me, I can go and find rest.

It isn't an easy place to find, especially in today's hectic world. When I was little, I remember crawling up on my daddy's lap and feeling his protecting arm around me. At first, I would snuggle up to him, taking such joy in his love for me. But, not too long, and I would be squirming to get down. If he had already fallen asleep, that was easy. But sometimes he would say, "stop squirming and rest a little longer. You'll feel so much better if you do."

And now, though my earthly father has gone to his home in heaven, I can hear my Father say those same words to me: "Abide in me child and you will feel so much better."

THE PLACE OF SWEET ABIDING

Lord, take me to the place of sweet abiding
As the clouds float in the sky
Not afraid of falling or rising too high
Nestled in the blueness
Content to go whichever way Your wind blows

Bring me in to Your sanctuary this morning, Lord
Take away every fear, every sadness
Fill me with the joy of Your Presence
I am nestled in the warmth of Your love
Send me where You desire me to go
I want to be in Your Spirit's control

If you obey my commands, you will remain in my love,
just as I have obeyed my Father's commands and remain
in his love. (John 15:10)

TO BE IN YOU

I spend so much time, Lord
In the unreality of this world
Among things that will not last
Being entrapped by emotions
Dependent upon situations
Which have no lasting significance

Do not take me out of this world
But help my soul to live above it

Therefore, I urge you, brothers, in view of God's mercy, to offer your bodies as living sacrifices, holy and pleasing to God—this is your spiritual act of worship. Do not conform any longer to the pattern of this world, but be transformed by the renewing of your mind. Then you will be able to test and approve what God's will is—his good, pleasing and perfect will. (Romans 12:1-2)

PRICELESS DAYS

Nonmoney making days
Days to rest and refresh
After such a hectic season

My heart rejoices
As I drink fully from Your fountain
Let me be found in You
Wherever I am, whatever time of day
Indeed, You ARE the grace that I walk in
There is none besides You
NO ONE can give such love, such grace
NO ONE has authority to impute righteousness
To sinful creatures such as I
Only in Your blood, by Your blood
Only by the power of Your resurrection
Your mercies are new every morning
Let Your glory fill the temple, Lord
You are my God
Since I was a young child
Forever You will be
My God
I love You so very much

I pray also that the eyes of your heart may be enlightened in order that you may know the hope to which he has called you, the riches of his glorious inheritance in the saints, and his incomparably great power for us who believe. That power is like the working of his mighty strength, which he exerted in Christ when he raised him from the dead and seated him at his right hand in the heavenly realms. (Ephesians 1:18-20)

GOD'S WORLD

A burst of bright colors
The brilliance of which I've never seen
In this earthly life
One by one appearing
A bright blue butterfly flutters past a sparkling yellow sun
The burning red flowers dance under snow white clouds
I will stay in this world forever
Forever with You, God
Abiding in You
Living so that every moment is enhanced, magnified
Made brilliant by Your very Presence
You are an awesome God
To let me see into Your world

*I have seen you in the sanctuary and beheld your power
and your glory. Because your love is better than life, my
lips will glorify you. I will praise you as long as I live, and in
your name I will lift up my hands. My soul will be satisfied
as with the richest of foods; with singing lips my mouth
will praise you. (Psalm 63:2-5)*

WHERE MY HEART LIVES

The place beyond weakness
Beyond fear
Beyond death
That is where my heart lives

The place where Jesus reigns
Where there are no tears
Beyond rejection
Beyond sin
Beyond pain
That is where my heart lives
Oh the rest in this wonderful place
Where no evil dwells

*From the ends of the earth I call to you, I call as my heart
grows faint; lead me to the rock that is higher than I. For
you have been my refuge, a strong tower against the foe.
I long to dwell in your tent forever and take refuge in the
shelter of your wings. Selah*
*For you have heard my vows, O God; you have given me
the heritage of those who fear your name. (Psalm 61:2-5)*

THE BASKET CASE

Nerves fraught, on edge
Waking up with a full slate
Of irritation and an overwhelming feeling
That everything is not in place

I come to Your throne
As a fragile, near basket case
And I drink in Your beauty
The ointment of Your Holy Spirit
Heals me
The music taking me to the place
Where You are
A place where everything is set right
And You alone are in control

Let me walk in Your peace
All day long, sweet Jesus
Turn every irritation into an
Opportunity to give thanks
Let me rest in Your plans for me
Taking joy in every unexpected moment

Come to me, all you who are weary and burdened, and I will give you rest. Take my yoke upon you and learn from me, for I am gentle and humble in heart, and you will find rest for your souls. (Matthew 11:28-29)

THE WINGS

They are so awesome, Lord
The wings that surround me
Oh, the warmth of being enfolded, protected
So close to the heart of God
They are so strong, Lord
Taking all the pressure that once was on me
Taking all the blows
All the strife
All the pain
I curl up under your wings
And rejoice in their protection
They are so soft, Lord
I could reach out and touch the softness
But I don't have to
It touches me
Comfort, grace, oh the deep love
The tenderness in those wings

On my bed I remember you; I think of you through the watches of the night. Because you are my help, I sing in the shadow of your wings. My soul clings to you; your right hand upholds me. (Psalm 63:6-8)

MORE OF YOU

As a baby chick opens its beak
To receive nourishment from its mother
My mouth is open wide
Eyes dimly seeing
The light of Your glory
My heart is empty of myself
A vessel awaiting Your filling
More of You, Jesus!

Open your mouth wide and I will fill it. (Psalm 81:10)

MY HEART

Even before I was born
Your eyes were upon me
You formed my heart
The softness of it
The vulnerability
In me
You put a deep desire
A desperate longing
For You
And You continued
To fill that longing
Each year of my life
How I look forward
To growing closer to You
In the years to come

For you created my inmost being; you knit me together in my mother's womb. I praise you because I am fearfully and wonderfully made; your works are wonderful, I know that full well. My frame was not hidden from you when I was made in the secret place. When I was woven together in the depths of the earth, your eyes saw my unformed body. All the days ordained for me were written in your book before one of them came to be. (Psalm 139:13-16)

JESUS, MY LIFE

Jesus Christ, you are my life
The very breath I breathe
You are my energy
When I wake
My rest when I sleep
You are the sparkle in my eyes
And the glistening of my tears
I am in You and You are in me
Abiding, living, renewing
Rejoicing
How can I lose today when You are with me?

For to me, to live is Christ and to die is gain. (Philippians 1:21)

THE MEETING

With a smile on my lips
And a leap of joy in my heart
I settle down to meet with You, God
The Almighty One, Conqueror of the Universe
Desires my company!
It is too wonderful for words
Oh, the blessed assurance
To know You are here
To know You are real!
To feel Your love surround me
Lifting me up above all my worries
Taking all my burdens
As Your own
Wonderful Father
I rest in You this morning

Yet I am not ashamed, because I know whom I have believed, and am convinced that he is able to guard what I have entrusted to him for that day. (2 Timothy 1:12)

IN THE MIST

The beautiful lake lies in the valley
Surrounded by mountains
And covered with mist
My heart and what's beautiful in it
Lies still
Covered with a mist
Coming from...
Where?
I long for the Sonshine to break through
Shining and reflecting His own glory
I long to see who I really am
Not fettered by tears
And yet, in the valley
Surrounded by mountains
And covered with mist
I know God's presence
He is real
He is near
Silent and calm
Waiting, Teaching,
Bringing peace

I cried out to God for help; I cried out to God to hear me. When I was in distress, I sought the Lord; at night I stretched out untiring hand and my soul refused to be comforted. Then I thought, "To this I will appeal: the years of the right hand of the Most High." I will remember the deeds of the LORD; yes, I will remember your miracles of long ago. I will meditate on all your works and consider all your mighty deeds. Your ways, O God, are holy. What god is so great as our God? You are the God who performs miracles; you display your power among the peoples. (Psalm 77:1-2, 10-14)

CLOSE TO YOU

To touch the wind
And know that You are there
To smell the rain
And take in Your Presence
To view the sunset
As if seeing the glory of God
Make its way to the other side
Of the world
What a privilege it is
To live always
In Your Presence

Through the victories you gave, his glory is great; you have bestowed on him splendor and majesty. Surely you have granted him eternal blessings and made him glad with the joy of your presence. For the king trusts in the LORD; through the unfailing love of the Most High he will not be shaken. (Psalm 21:5-7)

MIRACLES IN YOU

You showed them miracles
Yet they turned to the mundane
You parted the waters
Yet some chose to drown with the chariots
You led them with cloud and fire
Yet they chose to listen to their inner voices…
"Wouldn't it be more fun in Egypt?"

There is NO path but Yours
There is no life apart from You
There are no miracles
Except in You

Show me Your path, dear Director of my soul
Give me Your life, sweet Jesus
Do a great miracle for me, in me, today
O God, my help from ages past!

Psalm 78

YOUR GLORY

Show me Your glory, Lord
As Moses prayed, I pray, show me Your glory
The clean pure brightness of Your holiness
My heart's eyes protected by the blood of Jesus
Or else I would burn up in Your brightness

Show me Your glory, Lord
Overwhelm me with Your abounding love
Let me look into the depths of Your faithfulness
Eyes, pools of deep, deep love
Deeper than the deepest ocean
Wider than the widest sea

Show me Your glory, Lord
Answer my heart's cry to see You
"Blessed are the pure in heart for they shall see God"
No wonder You have been guiding me to pray for purity
You want me to see You

I look into Your holiness
O Lord, my God
And fall on my face

Then Moses said, "Now show me your glory." And the LORD said, "I will cause all my goodness to pass in front of you, and I will proclaim my name, the LORD, in your presence. I will have mercy on whom I will have mercy, and I will have compassion on whom I will have compassion. (Exodus 33:18-19)

MY HIDING PLACE

Lord, you are indeed my hiding place
Like the dove which set out to find a place to rest
But found none
I fly from my place of safety
Thinking I can find somewhere to rest my weary soul
But in the end
I always come back to You
And You put out Your hand
And bring me into the ark
In to Yourself
And there I find rest for my soul

You are my hiding place; you will protect me from trouble and surround me with songs of deliverance. Selah (Psalm 32:7)

DRAW ME TO YOURSELF

Here You are
Compelling me with gentle eyes
Drawing me to Yourself
With grace exuding from You
And penetrating the deepest parts of my soul
Your hands extending, beckoning
But not pulling

I come to You
To fall at Your feet
To kiss Your nail-scarred hands
I will wet those scars with my tears
And dry them with my hair
You have drawn me to Yourself with grace
And in Your Presence
I will abide

When a woman who had lived a sinful life in that town learned that Jesus was eating at the Pharisee's house, she brought an alabaster jar of perfume, and as she stood behind him at his feet weeping, she began to wet his feet with her tears. Then she wiped them with her hair, kissed them and poured perfume on them. (Luke 7:37-38)

THE HECTIC DAY

Take me to some sweet place today, O Lord
A place of perfect peace
And quiet rest
Under the shadow of Your wings
I wait, until Your Spirit hides me
Enfolds me, rests me in His arms
The days speed by
As though racing to some end
Which would kill me
But I rest in you
Starting with this morning
In the quiet place
Each new task today
I will embrace with open arms
Full attention, unspeakable joy
Because I am not grasping for rest
Or searching for a moment to myself
In my heart, the place that matters
I will be with You
And You in me
All throughout this busy day

Your righteousness is like the mighty mountains, your justice like the great deep. O LORD, you preserve both man and beast. How priceless is your unfailing love! Both high and low among men find refuge in the shadow of your wings. They feast on the abundance of your house; you give them drink from your river of delights. (Psalm 36:6-8)

AN ENCOUNTER

(Written overlooking the harbor in Kobe, Japan)

The soft cool breeze kisses my skin
A touch of the Holy One
Sun shining upon the water
Smile drops from the Savior
Sparkling in the deep, like diamonds
Waiting to be harvested
I feel Your love
I see Your love

How beautiful is the city behind me
Let Your Spirit ignite Your people, Lord
Let them feel the softness of Your love
The beauty in Your smile
And as the sparkles in the water
Stir in me a desire for You
Let the glory on the faces of Your children
Entice those who are still in darkness
Bringing them into an encounter
They have never had before

The LORD appeared to us in the past, saying: "I have loved you with an everlasting love; I have drawn you with loving-kindness. (Jeremiah 31:3)

Identity

I believe all of us go through periods of time when we wonder who we are; what is our purpose; will we leave a mark on the world? At some times in our lives, those questions become more troublesome. God has always been there to answer the questions of my heart, as elementary or juvenile, as they may seem. He shows me who I am in Him, and that is a very good thing to know!

When I know who I am, I am more likely to see others with the eyes the Father gives me. Eyes of love and not insecurity; eyes of grace and not judgment; eyes of humility and not self-righteous pride.

THE ANCHOR OF MY SOUL

The boat lies silent and still upon the soundless lake
Alone
Sail wrapped tightly and tethered to its resting place
No free flying right now
Resting in its solace
Beautiful boat silhouetted by the sunrise
Alone
Not swaying back and forth
Gently turning round for me
To see the buoy and strong rope
Which ties her to the anchor
Which surely lies at the bottom of the dark waters
The anchor, which keeps her steady
Awaiting the purpose for which she was made

God did this so that, by two unchangeable things in which it is impossible for God to lie, we who have fled to take hold of the hope offered to us may be greatly encouraged. We have this hope as an anchor for the soul, firm and secure. It enters the inner sanctuary behind the curtain, where Jesus, who went before us, has entered on our behalf. He has become a high priest forever, in the order of Melchizedek. (Hebrews 6:18-20)

WHAT IS LIFE?

Life is not a series of tasks
To be accomplished
Check this one off the list
Add it to the 'I feel good about myself' list
Check this one off with half a check
Not done so well, mistakes all through it
Add it to the 'you're a failure' list
And so the tasks continue day after day
One checklist to another
Wad it up, crumpled paper
That represents who I am and what I'm worth
Lies! Lies! Lies!

Life is not a series of tasks
To be judged
One accomplishment after another
Meeting with the Father's measuring stick

Life is walking in free and open spaces
The wind of the Spirit
Filling me
And taking me to heights I've never known before
Life is the beating of my heart
To the rhythm of the dance of the ages

It is the passion which frees me
To do and be far beyond the words I could write
On my list

It is the knowledge of the timeless One
Walking in Him—in eternity
Feeling Him, Enjoying Him
Singing in the timeless place
Unbound, unfettered, free

It is for freedom that Christ has set us free. Stand firm, then, and do not let yourselves be burdened again by a yoke of slavery. (Galations 5:1)

ONLY YOU, JESUS

You are the author of my soul
The Creator of every line
Every word, every syllable
Carefully placed
Every stroke scripted into beauty
Starting first in Your mind's eye
In the secret places of Your heart
My life, flowing from Your pen
As the ink on this page flows out of my heart
May all the letters of my life
Be of Your choosing
May every syllable mark
The weight of your hand
May the Words of my life
Be strong and sure
Soft and gentle
Only You, Jesus

This is the covenant I will make with them after that time, says the Lord. I will put my laws in their hearts, and I will write them on their minds." Then he adds: "Their sins and lawless acts I will remember no more." (Hebrews 10:16-17)

You show that you are a letter from Christ, the result of our ministry, written not with ink but with the Spirit of the living God, not on tablets of stone but on tablets of human hearts. (2 Corinthians 3:3)

YOUR EYES

Give me Your eyes, dear Father
To see the people in this world
Black or white, Hispanic or Jew
High-school dropout or executive
Lying hypocrite
Or doped up, battered, abused, abandoned prostitute
The seed of Your thoughts
The apple of Your eye
Created in Your image
Each with the potential
To be changed and to change
Some corner of their world

Give my Your eyes, Father God
To separate the sin from the sinner
To look at someone face to face
And see right through
To their heart
To hate evil
But to bring redemption
To stand for righteousness
But to breathe humility
To never compromise
Yet keep a soft heart

As I gaze into Your quiet face
I am lost in Your eyes
As deep as the universe
So full of love
For me
The greatest of sinners
You gaze at me
In the weakness of my humanity
And You infuse me with power
You resurrect me from my brokenness
And send me forth
With eyes as deep as the universe
So full of love
For all I see

Jesus looked at him and loved him. "One thing you lack,"
he said. "Go, sell everything you have and give to the
poor, and you will have treasure in heaven. Then come,
follow me." (Mark 10:21)

WHO I AM IN YOU

You say to me,
"I am tired
I am sad
I am depressed"
You come to me
Complaining about what is making you the way
You are
But I say to you
"I am the great I AM"
There is nothing
That you could be
That is greater than me
Or that I AM in you
I AM greater
Than your sadness
I AM stronger
Than your pain
I AM bigger
Than your depression
Let me BE
Let me be your peace
Let me be your joy
Let me be your healing
In Me, you are beautiful

Ah, Sovereign LORD, you have made the heavens and the earth by your great power and outstretched arm. Nothing is too hard for you. "I am the LORD, the God of all mankind. Is anything too hard for me?" (Jeremiah 32:17,27)

LET THERE BE LIGHT

He speaks light into my darkness
The Word enters the realm of man
And splits the curtain
So that I may see His righteousness
Oh, the glory of His light
His righteousness penetrates
The darkest corner
Shattering the smallest pieces
Your righteousness flows over me
Making me right before You

And God said, "Let there be light," and there was light.
(Genesis 1:3)

CAN'T STEAL MY JOY

Jesus, You are my power
To defeat the enemy who says
You don't really love me
Who puts doubts in my mind
And self pity in my heart
I climb back on your lap my gracious Father
And together we fight the one
Who would steal my joy and witness
Let me feel Your loving arms around me!

Finally, brothers, whatever is true, whatever is noble, whatever is right, whatever is pure, whatever is lovely, whatever is admirable—if anything is excellent or praiseworthy—think about such things. (Philippians 4:8)

BIRTHDAY GIFTS

Lord, You have made me
You know me
Every limp, every potential
Cancerous spot
Every black spot of self-deceit
Lord, You know me
You fashioned me
You know every sign of beauty in me
You know my talents
My tenderness
You know my love for You
And You love me

With a depth I cannot fathom
Your light shines deep into my soul
O what beauty
That You should fill me so
The light of Your smile
Your love warming me up
Even in the coldest places
How I thank You for these
Birthday gifts!
Jesus, lover of my soul!

O LORD, you have searched me and you know me. You know when I sit and when I rise; you perceive my thoughts from afar. You discern my going out and my lying down; you are familiar with all my ways. Before a word is on my tongue you know it completely, O LORD. (Psalm 139: 1-4)

STANDING STRONG

Roots sunk deep in rich dark soil
Spread thick, holding firm
From generation to generation
Your deeds of righteousness
And mighty acts support me
Giving me a base to grow on
Shooting high into the air
Branches firm and strong
Not with boughs beaten down
From wind and rain

You lift me up when I fall
Your power makes me stand tall
Forever and ever, eternally
Standing tall to praise You
Looking to You as the fulfiller
Of all my desires
Calling to You in truth and love
I know You hear me
You promised and You are faithful

*He is like a tree planted by streams of water, which
yields its fruit in season and whose leaf does not wither.
Whatever he does prospers. (Psalm 1:3)*

94

MY INHERITANCE

I am chosen for Your kingdom
And You are my inheritance
I am part of a priesthood of believers
Praise You, God, I will never feel cheated
Put upon, unblessed
You are my inheritance
If You said, "I give you the moon, the stars
and the universe"
It would not be worth what I already possess
If You said, "I will crown you and make you
Pastor of many"
It would not be better than the position I have in Christ
already
I belong to You and You are mine
My inheritance
Which will never rot away, blow away
Or be taken away from me

*But you are a chosen people, a royal priesthood, a holy
nation, a people belonging to God, that you may declare
the praises of him who called you out of darkness into his
wonderful light. (1 Peter 2:9)*

MY ROLE

The lessons I am learning now
Are not of my choosing
Although I prayed
"Lord, never give up on me
Until I am formed in the image of Your Son"
I didn't know there was so much pride left
I never thought I had so much further to go
Learning to be a servant leader is one thing
When you are looked up to and admired
When it is a joy to do the work

It is another thing
When the tasks are uncomfortable
And unsightly
Gaining no praise or recognition
It is not easy to pray
That I will do whatever you've given me to do
When what You have called me to
Is to be a support
The beam which holds up the roof
The orchestrator of the background music
But, oh, Lord
I see now the desperate importance of those roles
There would be no roof, save for the beam

There would be no song without the background music

Thank you for never giving up on me Lord

And we know that in all things God works for the good of those who love him, who have been called according to his purpose. For those God foreknew he also predestined to be conformed to the likeness of his Son, that he might be the firstborn among many brothers. (Romans 8:28-29)

YOUR SERVANT

Allow me to be your servant, Lord
Not a great and mighty scholar
Not a well known pianist or speaker
But your servant
In the eyes of the Japanese
One who is humble
Willing to learn
Ever growing
Changing
Becoming
And yet
One who is strong in the Word
One who's roots go deep
And whose foundation is solid
Never changing
Never fearing
Ever faithful

Jesus called them together and said, "You know that the rulers of the Gentiles lord it over them, and their high officials exercise authority over them. Not so with you. Instead, whoever wants to become great among you must be your servant, and whoever wants to be first must be your slave— just as the Son of Man did not come to be served, but to serve, and to give his life as a ransom for many." (Matthew 20:25-28)

THE CHILD

Undeserving child that I am
You lavish on me
Grace upon grace
Wayward, sinful, lazy
Daughter that I am
You cherish me
With tender eyes of mercy
Faltering, fumbling, stumbling
Toddler that I am
You penetrate my soul
With Almighty power
And infuse me with hope to go on
Cherished, adored, strengthened
I am a child of the great I AM

Yet to all who received him, to those who believed in his name, he gave the right to become children of God— children born not of natural descent, nor of human decision or a husband's will, but born of God. (John 1:12-13)

WHAT DO YOU SEE?

When You look at me, Lord
You see a reflection of Yourself
Wonderfully, uniquely sparkling in me
You see a woman
Complete in You
Beautiful in You
A shining diamond
Every facet of which
Magnifies Your face
Your glory shines on me
And colors radiate all around
Reds of love
Yellows of joy
Blues of compassion
All adding up to a rainbow of hope
Lord, Help me to always see myself
As You see me

All beautiful you are, my darling; there is no flaw in you.
(Song of Songs 4:7)

IN YOUR EYES

I love the way I look in Your eyes
A reflection of Your beautiful Son
Clothed in robes of righteousness
Bringing to You a sweet fragrance

The world may see me differently
So many filters
Dirtied by their own hurts and scars
Marred views because of what I once was
Or slips of the tongue I have made

But I love the way I look in Your eyes
A bride prepared for her beloved
Not one blemish, not one scar
Not one piece of dirt

I do not always see myself as You see me
Bitter thoughts rise in my heart
The strangle hold of what is now
Obstructs the beauty of what is to be

Give me Your eyes, forever and always, Lord
Let me see and believe in myself
As You see and believe in me
A glorious work in You

When you were dead in your sins and in the uncircumcision of your sinful nature, God made you alive with Christ. He forgave us all our sins, having canceled the written code, with its regulations, that was against us and that stood opposed to us; he took it away, nailing it to the cross. (Colossians 2:13-14)

TO SPEAK LIKE GOD

Oh the depth of Your wisdom
And knowledge of Your creation
To know all our needs
All our desires
The rate of our growth
Oh, the beautiful artistry
Of not only revealing the right words
But leaving even precious words unsaid
Because it was not the time or place
To throw Your pearls before swine.

Only with complete reliance on Your Spirit, Lord
Will my lips speak like Yours
Only when Your heart becomes mine
Will I be able to see into the hearts of those I teach
Only when I give Your mind complete control in me
Will I be able to give forth wisdom
Give me Your Spirit Jesus, Your heart, Your mind
So that I may teach others the wonders of Your kingdom

When Jesus had finished saying these things, the crowds were amazed at his teaching, because he taught as one who had authority, and not as their teachers of the law. (Matthew 7:28-29)

BEING ME

Bathed in the light of Your grace
Sunshine and warmth
Mingling together and
Keeping me
Pure, protected
Beautiful
Your light, Your truth
Exposing all the darkness
Bringing out the best in me
The "me" that You intended
To create
The one who is made perfect
In You
The one You are perfecting
In the light of Your grace
I will walk
And celebrate the fact
That all I do
Is done through You!

*(I am) confident of this, that he who began a good work
in you will carry it on to completion until the day of Christ
Jesus. (Philippians 1:6)*

TRANSFORMATION

We are born for beauty
Changed from the ugliness of sin
To experience a butterfly transformation
Let our art be transformed
From obscene and ludicrous
To holy and meaningful
Let our music be transformed, Lord
From loud cries of sharp-edged tones
To notes bathed in Holy Spirit joy
Notes that give life
No replicas from satan to fill this place
Pure, God-given holy beauty
The beauty of righteousness

*I will give thanks to the LORD because of his righteousness
and will sing praise to the name of the LORD Most High.
(Psalm 7:17)*

*They will celebrate your abundant goodness and joyfully
sing of your righteousness. (Psalm 145:7)*

HOLY OF HOLIES

I cannot run, Lord
My knees are too weak
I cannot walk
My heart is too weary
Carry me into the Holy of Holies

I am not worthy, Lord
My doubts are too great
I don't deserve Your glory, Lord
The stain of my sin is too black
Bring me into the Holy of Holies

Light of glory
Red blood of innocence
Never weary or tired
God of all faithfulness
Bring me into the Holy of Holies

Refresh my parched soul
With the living water
Which gushes through
The streets of gold
Where Your Presence fills
The Holy of Holies

Undeserving, weak and trembling
I stand before Your Holy Presence
And drink in the mystery
That one such as I
Could be standing in the Holy of Holies

Therefore, brothers, since we have confidence to enter the Most Holy Place by the blood of Jesus, by a new and living way opened for us through the curtain, that is, his body, and since we have a great priest over the house of God, let us draw near to God with a sincere heart in full assurance of faith, having our hearts sprinkled to cleanse us from a guilty conscience and having our bodies washed with pure water. Let us hold unswervingly to the hope we profess, for he who promised is faithful. (Hebrews 10:19-23)

HOUSE WORK, HEART WORK

There are unironed shirts on the start of this New Year
But my heart is pressed into Your mold
There are scattered papers and 3-year-old magazines
But Your Word is on my tongue and penetrates my soul
There are unmade beds and junky closets
But your Spirit searches every part of me
And puts the things that concern me in order
There are way too many pounds clinging to me
But You cut off the excess in my soul
And give me strength to do
What You are calling me to do

I let go of the things I cannot control
I let your love control all of me

For God did not give us a spirit of timidity, but a spirit of
power, of love and of self-discipline. (2 Timothy 1:7)

CHANGED

I am comforted by Your peace
I am warmed by Your love
I am awed by Your compassion
I am blown away by Your greatness
But I am changed by Your holiness
As I sit in Your righteousness
All that is ugly in me
Disappears
And I see myself in Your image
As You have made me to be!

"Who among the gods is like you, O LORD? Who is like you— majestic in holiness, awesome in glory, working wonders?" (Exodus 15:11)

Growth

Sometimes, from the place where we are standing, it doesn't seem as though much growth has taken place in our lives. As Christians, we wrestle with the same problems we had years ago. We pray the same prayers, ask for the same deliverances, and read over the same verses. But then God gives us a panoramic view of where we have come from. He shows us the experiences He has brought us through. He gives us an "ah ha" moment that says, "Yes God! I see the work You have done in me. You promised to perfect what concerns me and You have done it, are doing it." And we realize again, we are works in progress. The progress might seem especially slow at times, but God never gives up!

LIFE IN THE TUMBLER

The precious gem of my soul
Lies deep in my heart
Hidden under crusts, layers and layers
Of selfishness, sinfulness and ugliness
The tumbler churns
Circumstances all wonderfully
Orchestrated by Your mighty hand
The tumbler, Your word
Never changing, penetrating
Rock solid
"Love the Lord Your God...
Love Your neighbor...
Abhor evil and cling to what is good...
Take up your cross...
Fear the Lord...
Worship the Lord...
Trust the Lord
The tumbler stops "I've got it Lord! The gems are
showing now Lord!"
But wait, only a tiny shining piece
Peeking through the hard crust
The circumstances change
Again marvelously arranged
By Your gentle hand

And the tumbler begins again
"Love the Lord Your God…
Love your neighbor

But Lord, I've heard this before
And yet, it is like I'm seeing it for the first time
The precious gem of my soul
Tumbles in different directions now
Polishing the smooth, shiny surface
Chipping away at the ugliness
Yes, Lord, I think I've got it now
I understand what it means
I can do it right this time
And the circumstances change
Again
Not by happenstance or some
Whimsical caprice of a malicious God
But by the tender and tough
Love of the one who created me
And is creating me
The tumbler begins again
Love the Lord your God
Love your neighbor…
Abhor what is evil…
Take up your cross…

Lord, I thought I understood
But now I don't know
What would you teach me?
Where is the finish of this depth?
When will I ever understand?
I want to do it right
But I can't
Help me!
And the circumstances change again
With such foresight, such knowledge
Such tenderness
And the tumbler rolls
Again
Love the Lord your God
Love Him, love Him, love Him

Worship Him
Trust Him
Follow him
Serve Him
Love Him!!
Lord, I may never understand it all
But teach me
I may never know the depth
Of all that You are
And all that You want of me

I trust You
To do it right in me
Let the circumstances change
That I might experience Your grace
In a different light
Let the tumbler churn
The precious gem is not my own
It is a diamond of Your making
Make it shine in every facet
For You alone!

Therefore, my dear friends, as you have always obeyed—not only in my presence, but now much more in my absence—continue to work out your salvation with fear and trembling, for it is God who works in you to will and to act according to his good purpose. (Philippians 2:12-13)

LIFE IN THE TUMBLER CONTINUED... 20 YEARS LATER

Again the circumstances change
And God says:
"Work it out, work it out!
Apply your faith even now
As you feel your world caving in
As the waters crash around you
And all your dreams are undone
Keep up with virtue
Don't give in to angry eruptions
Or unkind words
Continue knowing Me
And desiring to know Me
Keep on hungering after Me
You can never have enough of Me
Or know all of me

Let me work out self-control for you
In these circumstances over which
You have no control
Don't give up
Yes, you have worked it out before
But this is different
Yet I am the same

I am with you as I was in going to Japan
In the earthquake and the fire
And coming back to America
I will help you persevere
Don't give up
Continue to desire godliness
Be kind, even if you don't feel like it
Be kind and love
I will fill you with all my love
My oceans are deep
And the source never dries up
Drink from Me my child
You're gonna make it
I promise!"
God

Let us not become weary in doing good, for at the proper time we will reap a harvest if we do not give up. Therefore, as we have opportunity, let us do good to all people, especially to those who belong to the family of believers. (Galations 6:9-10)

A PILGRIM

A solitary pilgrim
Yet not on a journey alone
Joined by countless others
Who believe in You
Our guide our instructor
Our companion
Guide me O Thou Great Jehovah
Pilgrim in this barren land
Lead me to new levels of discipline
New heights in prayer
New depths in faith

Therefore, since we are surrounded by such a great cloud of witnesses, let us throw off everything that hinders and the sin that so easily entangles, and let us run with perseverance the race marked out for us. Let us fix our eyes on Jesus, the author and perfecter of our faith, who for the joy set before him endured the cross, scorning its shame, and sat down at the right hand of the throne of God. (Hebrews 12:1-2)

TOO MUCH TO DO

I wish I could snap my fingers
And the clothes would be folded and in drawers
I wish I could twitch my nose
And the boxes would be unpacked
And everything in its proper place
Beautiful, smooth
The way it's supposed to be....
But I know better
One article at a time
One fork, one book,
One box at a time

That's the way it is
Inside me
One sin committed
And another and another
Until my heart is cluttered
Just as this house is...
No magic formula to put all in order quickly
But one at a time
A sin confessed, forgiveness received
Healing of the wounded spot
Another place revealed
Confessed, forgiven, healed

Until all is
Beautiful and smooth
The way it's supposed to be...

If we confess our sins, he is faithful and just and will forgive us our sins and purify us from all unrighteousness. (1John 1:9)

THE WILLOW

Long, thin, spindly branches
Antennae stretching high
Upward, reaching
Skeleton fingers, poking to the left and right
Overlapping, joining at the oddest places
A seemingly random pattern of weakness
Against the pale blue sky
Each stripped bare of any fine greenery
The wind blows, threatening to snap the branches
Into tiny pieces
But they are firmly fixed to the trunk
Hard and strong
Never blown by the wind
Firmly connected to the source
Of all nourishment
Its roots sapping up
All that the branches need
To live

God, You are the source of all my strength
All I need to live
I am so weak, so breakable
And yet…when I am fixed in Jesus
Nothing can harm me

The wind of You, Holy Spirit
Blows so gently at first
But then harder
Stripping me of all but the fact that I am in You
And that is enough to let me live
Connected to all of these other weak branches
Members of the same Jesus
Each weak, going different directions
But still striving to go upward
Joining together in praise to the
Father, Son, and Holy Spirit

The body is a unit, though it is made up of many parts;
and though all its parts are many, they form one body. So
it is with Christ. For we were all baptized by one Spirit into
one body—whether Jews or Greeks, slave or free—and
we were all given the one Spirit to drink.
(1 Corinthians 12:12-13)

GUILT

Oh sweet One, You have released me
From my guilt
Guilt over not doing
What I am not called to do
Guilt over not being
What I am not
Guilt over not meeting
Others' expectations
Some of which
Are only in my mind
You have indeed set my feet
In wide open spaces
And with pure freedom
I serve You
It is so refreshing
To look forward
To the day again

I care very little if I am judged by you or by any human court; indeed, I do not even judge myself. My conscience is clear, but that does not make me innocent. It is the Lord who judges me. Therefore judge nothing before the appointed time; wait till the Lord comes. He will bring to light what is hidden in darkness and will expose the motives of men's hearts. At that time each will receive his praise from God. (1 Corinthians 4:3-5)

MOLDABLE

He leaps onto my lap
Waiting for my strong arms
To mold him into the most comfortable position
Little head raised up to me
As if to say
"I'm here—love on me"
How can I resist
Pouring out my love
As his heart sighs in contented purrs

Sweet Father, I come to You this morning
Moldable, teachable
But there are parts of me still hard
Which threaten to take over
What has just been softened
Let all of me give in to Your touch, Jesus
Whatever it takes
Mold me with Your love
So that I might be all that You created me to be

*Yet, O LORD, you are our Father. We are the clay, you are
the potter; we are all the work of your hand. (Isaiah 64:8)*

OFF KEY DAY

Where can I go, Jesus?
The shadows follow me
Every note is off key
And the melody of my life is askew
Hold me close, dearest One
In the hour of my grief
You are indeed all I have
And You ask the question again
"Am I enough for you?"
Forgive me, Lord, for making the pursuit of my dreams
No matter how righteous
More important than You

But as for me, the nearness of God is my good; I have made the Lord GOD my refuge, That I may tell of all Your works. (Psalm 73:28 NASB)

THE PATH

The path God leads me on is never dull
Sometimes painful
Sometimes rough
But never dull
Even if the surroundings
Seem to never change
Each step is sure to bring a revelation
Of some kind or another

Perhaps it is the pebble inside my shoe
That causes me to have to wait
With skillful hands He shows me where to look
I examine and, Yappari (just as I thought)
There it is, the source of my pain
I was so busy
Hurrying down the path
I didn't want to stop
And wait
To take it out

Perhaps it is in the gait of my walk
That He reveals something to me
Or the number of needless steps
I take

As I rush to get to the end of the path
He reminds me:
The point is, getting somewhere
Is not the point
The going is

No, walking with the Lord
Is never dull
Sometimes painful, sometimes rough
But never dull

Trust in the LORD with all your heart and lean not on your own understanding; in all your ways acknowledge him, and he will make your paths straight. (Proverbs 3:5-6)

ARROW

Arrow of flint
Glinting face of steel
Fixed on the mark
Aimed with such surety and confidence
Steady and strong

Steel against steel
Mind challenging mind
Sharpening, honing
Making broad the base
While the point remains focused

Fire against steel
Invisible challenging substance
Refiners fire
Softening, strengthening
Purging of all impurity
So that, when the goal is reached
It will have been worth the effort

When the mark is hit
The victory will be in the
Beauty of the arrow and
Not the translucent power of the mark

I press on toward the goal to win the prize for which God has called me heavenward in Christ Jesus.
(Philippians 3:14)

Do you not know that in a race all the runners run, but only one gets the prize? Run in such a way as to get the prize. Everyone who competes in the games goes into strict training. They do it to get a crown that will not last; but we do it to get a crown that will last forever.
(1 Corinthians 9:24-25)

NEXT STEP

What is the next step, Lord?
I've never been here before
It seems dark but not unpleasant
I feel Your arms around me
Taking me through
Walking with me
Assuring me
I will wait on You
No matter how long it takes
Lead me on, blessed Savior

*The LORD will fulfill his purpose for me; your love, O
LORD, endures forever— do not abandon the works of
your hands. (Psalm 138:8)*

STRENGTH

Make me strong, Lord
Not a mealy mouthed whiner
Who is unpleasant to be around
Make me like Joseph
Who had hours in jail
To ponder the injustices done to him
Yet when he was released
He was truly
Free

The story of Joseph in jail. (Genesis 39-40)

TO SERVE YOU

Lord, I want to say I am made for better things
To speak Your words of light and wisdom
To sing Your songs of praise
And lead as others join
To play the notes that spring from my heart
Instead, this time, You lead me to wash feet
And dishes
And sheets
And counters and tables
You showed me again
That to serve others is to serve You
May You find me faithful
In whatever position You place me in
I love to serve You, Lord

Jesus called them together and said, "You know that the rulers of the Gentiles lord it over them, and their high officials exercise authority over them. Not so with you. Instead, whoever wants to become great among you must be your servant, and whoever wants to be first must be your slave— just as the Son of Man did not come to be served, but to serve, and to give his life as a ransom for many." (Matthew 20:25-28)

YOU ARE GOD

My fears
My doubts
My anger
Loom before me out of the mist
Clutching my heart and
Squeezing it until I can stand it
No longer

Where are you God?
Where is the victory You promised?
Day after Day
I catch a glimpse of your glory
But it is like a flickering light
Waiting to light up my life
But something, someone
Keeps blowing it out
Is it me, Lord?
Me?
The one who needs you most
Causing Your light to go out?
Engulfed by fears that cause me to forget that
You are the

All Powerful
All Mighty
Everlasting Father
Yes, my Father
Who cares for me

Father, these lessons I've been learning
Are hard to accept
I want smooth sailing
I don't want to have to
Think about sin in my life
Is there not an easier way
To chisel away the rough places?
No, I thought not
In that case, Lord,
Make me a willing vessel
One who can learn and change
Even though it means
Admitting I was wrong

Be still my soul
And know that
God is
God

"Be still, and know that I am God; I will be exalted among the nations, I will be exalted in the earth." (Psalm 46:10)

SERVING

I was hungry
The things of this world not satisfying my desire
And you fed me the Word of God
Which filled me

I was thirsty
My heart parched, dry and empty
And you gave me drink from the well of living water
And it quenched my thirst

I was a stranger
An outcast in my own community
Feeling unloved and unwanted
Yet you, a stranger to my country, invited me over
and took me into your heart

I was naked
My defenses down
My feelings raw and exposed by the trials of life
And you clothed me with the soothing ointment
of God's word

I was sick
Sick of my sinful self, disappointed, dejected
And you visited me
Bringing with you the medicine
Of forgiveness

I was in a prison
Of sin, jealousy and anger,
And you came to me
With freedom

For I was hungry and you gave me something to eat, I was thirsty and you gave me something to drink, I was a stranger and you invited me in, I needed clothes and you clothed me, I was sick and you looked after me, I was in prison and you came to visit me. (Matthew 25:35-36)

ON THE ANVIL

I said last week
"I am weary, Lord
Weary of being on the anvil
Weary of having people brought in to my life
To expose my heart problems
My pride
My selfishness
My desire to be in control"
I said last week
"Can't You let up a little while, Lord?
Let me bask in the glory of doing
Something well
Let me get caught up in the vision
Of what I will do for you?"
But you told me,
"It's the vision of Me that you should have
Discard your glory and your vision
And I will give You Myself."

Lord, don't take me off the anvil
Only when I'm ready to be used
Make me, shape me
Melt together the cracks that are deep down
Yes, Lord, I am still weary
But I will come to You
And You will give Me rest

In this you greatly rejoice, though now for a little while you may have had to suffer grief in all kinds of trials. These have come so that your faith—of greater worth than gold, which perishes even though refined by fire—may be proved genuine and may result in praise, glory and honor when Jesus Christ is revealed. Though you have not seen him, you love him; and even though you do not see him now, you believe in him and are filled with an inexpressible and glorious joy, for you are receiving the goal of your faith, the salvation of your souls. (1 Peter 1:6-9)

BLESSED

Blessed are those who mourn
For days that are lost
To selfishness and greed
For years that cannot be taken back
For wounds given and received

Blessed are those who mourn
For an obstinate and stubborn people
For those who cannot shed the old
And are afraid of the new
For those who limit God
And so cannot experience the fullness of His power

Blessed are those who mourn
Over a people lost in darkness
Chained to ungodly customs
Blinded by satan's angels
For the millions who, instead of mansions in heaven
Have made for themselves reservations in hell
But they don't know it

Blessed are those who mourn
For they shall be comforted
Their sorrow will be turned to gladness

The lost years will be restored
The glory and the power of the Lord
Will be revealed to them, in them

The world will see a great light
Through them
The Holy Spirit will be their double portion.
Amen and Amen!

Blessed are those who mourn, for they will be comforted.
(Matthew 5:4)

THE 23RD PSALM JB VERSION

Lord Jesus, You are my shepherd
When I don't know whether to go right or left
You whisper softly in my ear
When I am lying in the middle of the road
You gently prod me
"Keep going little one"
I shall not want
Because You provide for my every need
Along the way
Physically and emotionally
You give me grace and compassion
To give and give and give
WAY beyond what I feel
I am capable of
When I have run too hard and fall
Exhausted, irritable
Emotionally distraught
Into Your waiting arms
You give me rest
REAL rest
The kind that lets me wake up and say,
"I'm ready Lord.
Send me out again"
You ARE the restorer of my soul

And because You have restored my soul
I am able to follow You
On the paths of righteousness
Right living, doing the right thing
No matter what
No matter if I think the conversation is trivial, mundane
Not worth my time
No matter if my body is tired
Or my mind not focused
For Your name's sake
I am enabled to walk the paths of righteousness

Sometimes I feel like I am walking in the valley
Of the shadow of defeat
A gloominess I cannot penetrate
A sadness I cannot quell
An uneasiness I cannot pinpoint
Much less make quiet
But Your rod and Your staff
Your instruction, your counsel, your Spirit
YOU are with me
You embrace me at the deepest levels
Of who I am
You know me so much better than I know myself

You hear the deep sighing of regret in my soul
And You sigh with me
Then You say

"Come see the table I have prepared for you
In the presence of your enemies
Come, I know you are thirsty
Come and drink your fill
I know your soul is dehydrated
I know you are hungry for me
Come and I will fill you up to overflowing
I am going to anoint your head with oil"

I come to Your table, Lord
Your comfort, Your very Presence is so real
You fill all the dents and holes
Made by the assaults on my emotions this week
You embrace me and give me covering
So that the irritations I will face today
Cannot penetrate my joy
My heart is calm within me
Waiting for Your oil
Yes, Lord, my cup is running over
Yesterday, I felt like I was on empty
And this morning, I am filled to overflowing

Surely goodness and mercy will follow me today
And all the days of my life surely,
For sure, no pie-in-the-sky dream
I will dwell in your Presence forever

Psalm 23

NEW THINGS

New things
God creating something out of nothing
More out of less
Beauty out of ashes
Why must I analyze, justify, sanctify and set in stone
That which was before
"Do not remember the former things"
They are not sacred, nor unchangeable
Only I am unchangeable
Not WHAT I do, but Who I Am
I Will do something new
In you
Through you
With you

"Forget the former things; do not dwell on the past. See, I am doing a new thing! Now it springs up; do you not perceive it? I am making a way in the desert and streams in the wasteland. (Isaiah 43:18-19)

DO UNTO OTHERS

As I want others to do to me
Let me do to them, Lord
To look past my sometimes sour face
And see the tiredness
Or sadness
And understand the defenses I build
Around thoughts that have not been taken captive
To listen, truly listen
To my heart
As the words, inadequate or mistaken
Come from my mouth

Help me not to jump in so quickly to make my point
Just because I want to have the last word

Soften my heart today, Lord
Guard my mouth
Let my words bring peace
And love and joy
Gracious words to build and not tear down
Take over Jesus
I surrender this mind, all my thoughts
This heart, all my feelings
This body, all my weaknesses and strengths

This soul, every unique part of me
Love others through me

Do not let any unwholesome talk come out of your mouths, but only what is helpful for building others up according to their needs, that it may benefit those who listen. (Ephesians 4:29)

Suffering

When I began to hunger for the heart of the God, to know Him and to be like Him, I started praying "Lord, make me pure." I believed the words of Jesus: "Blessed are the pure in heart, for they shall see God." What I don't think I really believed, was that God would do anything needed to answer my prayer. He has taken me, my husband and family through some major rocky places in order to do the work in me for which I prayed.

At times, the pressure seemed so heavy that I wanted to take back my prayer. But as His Spirit worked within me, I realized that no amount of suffering will ever equal the joy I find in knowing Him. Nothing can replace the privilege I find in taking part in the sufferings of Christ.

STRUGGLES

The Lord said to me:
"The struggles you have been through
Are not in vain
It was necessary to teach you many things
Before the next step
Behold, I will come in glory
The glory of the Son of Man
Coming with the song of the angels
Wherever you are
I will be there
All the glory will be for Me

For My strength is perfected in weakness
I have made you weak
So that others will see Me
And not you
I will lift you up
At the proper time"

In this you greatly rejoice, though now for a little while you may have had to suffer grief in all kinds of trials. These have come so that your faith—of greater worth than gold, which perishes even though refined by fire—may be proved genuine and may result in praise, glory and honor when Jesus Christ is revealed. Though you have not seen him, you love him; and even though you do not see him now, you believe in him and are filled with an inexpressible and glorious joy, for you are receiving the goal of your faith, the salvation of your souls. (1 Peter 1:6-9)

THE FLOOD

The flood came to drown all that was good in me
Satan stood beside my road and blew His breath
So that the waters rose faster
The rain beat harder
Throwing in garbage all along the way
But You were there

You are the road
The pavement of my life
The waters cannot overwhelm me when I am with You
Or tear away the rock beneath my feet
Your breath, Oh God, picks me up
And tosses the garbage that satan throws in
Like tiny pieces of tissue
And the flood becomes a clear river
A river of Life
Flowing fast in places
White, exciting foam
Dancing over clean rocks
Rocks hewn from years of trials

Around the bend, the clear water flows silently
Slowly, gently
Others can bow their faces into the coolness
And be refreshed
Or jump into the depths
And be filled

*When you pass through the waters, I will be with you; and
when you pass through the rivers, they will not sweep
over you. When you walk through the fire, you will not be
burned; the flames will not set you ablaze. (Isaiah 43:2)*

GOD'S TEARS

*(Written for the parents of our daughter's friend who died
in a fire)*

Rain comes
Washing away the ashes
Hard rain, cleansing rain
Driving away the leaves deadened by smoke
And fire

No sunshine today
Only white fog hanging over the lake
Surrounding the mountains
Like a shroud
Tears from heaven fall over Mary's grave
Tears that bring life once again

Tears that make green
What once was thought dead
Tears that penetrate deep, dry cracks
Formed out of fire
But now becoming living streams
Tears of God
For the death of His precious one
And for the grief of His children

Just as the rain cleanses

And restores the earth

May your tears and our tears

Bring healing to your hearts

May God restore you to life

And put in you living streams

To carry you through

The dry and rough places

Precious in the sight of the LORD is the death of his saints.

(Psalm 116:15)

I CRY TO YOU

Holy, Almighty God!
You bend Your ear
To hear my feeble cry
Unable to belt it out
The whimper starts deep in my soul
At the first note of my cry
You hear me

Your arms reach out to take me in
No one can hear my voice like that
"Before there is a word on my tongue
Behold, You know it"
Your Spirit intercedes for me
With groans too deep for words
Your Words, Your Spirit, Your comfort
Filling my heart
Pushing out the cry
Which causes me such pain
The grief escapes me, Lord
Replace my mourning
With Your oil of joy
So that I might proclaim with all my strength
The greatness of my Savior!

In the same way, the Spirit helps us in our weakness. We do not know what we ought to pray for, but the Spirit himself intercedes for us with groans that words cannot express. (Romans 8:26)

THE DARKNESS

Smothering under a thick carpet of dark depression
Unable to see clearly
Or think about tomorrow
Only
"How am I going to get through
This next hour?"

Then they cried to the LORD in their trouble, and he saved them from their distress. He brought them out of darkness and the deepest gloom and broke away their chains. Let them give thanks to the LORD for his unfailing love and his wonderful deeds for men. (Psalm 107:13-15)

THE SEA

Let Your waves crash upon me, God
The power of them
Freeing my soul from barnacles
Which have attached themselves
While I chose to lay dormant
At the bottom of the sea

Get me to the top, Jesus
It may be frightening
Tumultuous, deafening
Heart-breaking
But I will see the sky again
As I submit my will to Yours

*Submit yourselves, then, to God. Resist the devil, and he
will flee from you. (James 4:7)*

ENDURANCE

The task is too big for me
My emotions too raw
The problems are too heavy for me
So, in defense
I shut my heart
And pretend I don't care
Or stoop to sarcastic words
Which are supposed to keep the pain
At arms length
But never do

I accept the pain, my own suffering Savior
I accept the loneliness
I accept the ill-fitting requirements
You have put upon me
I accept the criticism and lack of praise
I gladly choose to take part
In Your suffering
To give thanks in being allowed
To understand
In a very small part
What You endured for me

I want to know Christ and the power of his resurrection and the fellowship of sharing in his sufferings, becoming like him in his death. (Philippians 3:10)

SADNESS

Where can I go, Jesus?
The sadness follows me
From corner to corner
Of my mind
Every note is off key
And the melody of my life is askew
Hold me close, dearest One
In the hour of my grief
You are indeed all I have
And You ask the question again
"Am I enough for You?"
Forgive me, Lord, for making the pursuit of my dreams
No matter how righteous
More important than You

But whatever was to my profit I now consider loss for the sake of Christ. What is more, I consider everything a loss compared to the surpassing greatness of knowing Christ Jesus my Lord, for whose sake I have lost all things. I consider them rubbish, that I may gain Christ. (Philippians 3:7-8)

TESTS

Another test, another chapter to learn
The teacher, with skill and expertise
Fashions the test, not for the class
But for the student
With each heart, personality
And temperament in mind
He wisely puts together the exam
Not for the student to regurgitate
What has been fed to him
And leave, unchanged
But that what he has learned
Will be molded into him
A part of the new person
He is destined to become

*Now that I, your Lord and Teacher, have washed your feet,
you also should wash one another's feet. I have set you an
example that you should do as I have done for you. I tell
you the truth, no servant is greater than his master, nor is a
messengergreaterthantheonewhosenthim. (John 13:14-16)*

FAMILY

Warmth of the sunshine
Hearts stirred by melodies and often sung hymns
The voices of youth and of age
Blended in harmony
A blending of good
And not so good
Tension, yet support
Comfort in foundations long since laid
Of solid faith
Bringing oneness in spite of differences
Binding and bonding
The Solid Rock
Keeping all as one in spirit
If not in body or mind

Family
Bonds held strong in sickness or health
Poverty or wealth
Encouraging, giving again and again
Aware of waves that continue
Sometimes never ending
Smooth and calm
Other times engulfing
So there seems to be no way out

Knowing the presence of shifting sand
Yet always standing on
The Solid ground beneath

Family
We hold hands and jump the waves
Together

Therefore encourage one another and build each other up, just as in fact you are doing. (1 Thessalonians 5:11)

THE STONES

Bring some comfort to my soul, Oh Lord
It seems our afflictions
Have followed us so many years
Like stones along the creek bed
They lay
Not dissolving, not floating away
But as the water of Your Holy Spirit
Washes through the rivers of our lives
Those stones of suffering
Become gems whose beauty are beyond measure
Gems of faithfulness, endurance
Deliverance, patience, intercession
Given by the very hand of God
The pure life-giving water
Softens the jagged edges
And we can see Your face reflected
In each trial
Your hand upon each life
Your grace covering it all

I will rest by that stream, Lord
I do not have to make myself a bed
In pastures green
But beside the still waters
I will lay my head
On the stones You have fashioned for me

Genesis 28: 10-22

THE LIGHT

Sadness surrounding us
Darkness waiting at the crevice
Of the halfway open door
Waiting to destroy the light
Seeping in, unwanted
Unbidden, insidious
And cold

But I turn to the light
Which floods my soul
A light that has overcome the darkness
Once and for all
Again and again
Each day a victory
Over these jumbled emotions
Each day shining light
On what is real
And what is not
Each day driving out the demons
Which seek to torment our souls
With lies
I have no greater friend than You
No stronger ally!

You are my lamp, O LORD; the LORD turns my darkness into light. (2 Samuel 22:29)

THE DEPTHS OF YOUR PAIN

I do not know the depths of your pain
You will not let me in
Only the sad notes of a melancholy refrain
Give me a hint of the dark hole
In your heart
I am at peace
Knowing that your song
Reaches the Holy of holies
I cannot mend the broken fences
Or chase out the demons
But He can
And that's why you turn to Him
Someday perhaps you will be able
To lift me up with the song of victory
He is giving you now

Cast your cares on the LORD and he will sustain you; he will never let the righteous fall. (Psalm 55:22)

ALL YOU NEED

When the fire threatens to
Melt your shield of faith
When sorrow seems to
Drain every ounce of strength
May Jehovah be your rock

When the pain washes over you
Until you can see no more
May God be your eyes

When anger grips your heart
And threatens to strangle all that is good
May God be your goodness
He is all we need

The LORD is my rock, my fortress and my deliverer; my
God is my rock, in whom I take refuge. He is my shield
and the horn of my salvation, my stronghold. (Psalm 18:2)

Prodigals

Although I have never wandered far from God since I accepted Jesus as my Savior at nine, many years ago I began to realize there is not as much difference between the elder brother and the prodigal as I had once believed. Both need the Father's love, both should want to please only Him, both have ugly places they try to hide, both choose to run away... one in work and the other in play.

The Father waits for each of them to come to their senses and quit pointing the finger. He desires them to search their own hearts and find what is keeping them from receiving all that He wants to give. He wants them both to enjoy a deep, fulfilling relationship with Him. Father God waits to bestow all His treasure on His most beloved creation, no matter how far they have wandered from Him.

PRISONS

Some people's prisons you can see
Dark set eyes, pools of death
Slaves to sadness
The bars of addiction hiding the life
Choking out love and peace and joy
Some people's prisons you can see
By the hanging of the head
The drooping of the shoulders
The sunshine gone from eyes or face or walk

Other prisons are not so easily detected
Hidden behind fake smiles
And nice words
Bars decorated with morality
All the time surrounding
Some deep dark secret of the heart

O bondage Breaker
Won't you come and set us free!
Please do not let us rot in our cells
Until we become so used to the dark dankness
That we desire it more than
Fresh breezes and sunshine

Make a clean sweep of my life, Jesus
Down to the cobwebs in the corner
Lord, how we need Your grace

The Spirit of the Lord is on me, because he has anointed me to preach good news to the poor. He has sent me to proclaim freedom for the prisoners and recovery of sight for the blind, to release the oppressed, to proclaim the year of the Lord's favor. (Luke 4:18-19)

HOPE

(From the story of Hagar in Genesis 21)

Not a hope to go on
Not a word to stand on
No drop of clear pure water
To bathe the wounds in her soul
Lying in her desert
She cries out to anyone but the One who can help her
"Why?" she cries in agony
Railing against the One who promises
To make streams in the desert
Cursing the very Word which would give her life
Disregarding the hope He would put within her
The hope that would become
The anchor of her soul

*We have this hope as an anchor for the soul, firm and
secure. It enters the inner sanctuary behind the curtain,
where Jesus, who went before us, has entered on our
behalf. He has become a high priest forever, in the order
of Melchizedek. (Hebrews 6:19-20)*

THE CONTRAST

Padded softness, cushions of warmth
Wrapped in security
Knowing who I am
And whose I am
Taking sustenance from the never ending flow
The umbilical chord of the Holy Spirit
Developed human
A baby in God's arms
Ever receiving the life-giving force

The harshness of a world without
Without warmth, without light
Without God
Sharp edges that brutally cut
An exhilarating roller coaster ride
That gives bruises and whiplash
And lasts ten seconds
Living, or rather existing
From high to high

Life with the Father
The warmth of His light and glory
The exhilaration of being in the Presence
Of the King of Kings

Continuous living, abundant, exciting adventures
With God Almighty
Heart still cocooned in security
Life being lived to the fullest
Watching to see what good things
The Father will bring about today

Heart filled with shame and blame
God did it to me
My parents did it to me
My boss…. My school…. My friends
Anger festering, resentment, bitterness
Looking for ways to drown out the sorrow
That comes from lack of repentance
Take the smoke
Soothe the pain
Ease the mind
Don't think about tomorrow or yesterday
Lost in oblivion
Lost in unreality
Lost

Taste and see that the Lord is good!
Not just for two hours, but forever

Think about yesterday
All forgiven
Think about tomorrow
All in God's hands
Live today as a victorious Child of the King!

That if you confess with your mouth, "Jesus is Lord," and believe in your heart that God raised him from the dead, you will be saved. For it is with your heart that you believe and are justified, and it is with your mouth that you confess and are saved. (Romans 10:9-10)

Taste and see that the LORD is good; blessed is the man who takes refuge in him. (Psalm 34:8)

VISION OF HELL AND HEAVEN

Naked animals
Huddled together against the penetrating light
The light of the glory of Christ
Shaggy, dirty faces hid in shame
Cowering under the gaze of the Almighty
Muscled, strong backs
Turned away from the source of life
Buckled in tense anticipation of burning fire
Bent over under the weight of their filthiness

Child of God
Standing in the warmth of the glorious light
Face held high
Gazing upward toward the Source
Clothed in fine raiment
Flooded with the light
Cleansed by the light
Engulfed in the joy of the glorious moment
Having accepted the cross
No more afraid
Waiting in rapturous anticipation
Of the coming of the mighty King

Remember that at that time you were separate from Christ, excluded from citizenship in Israel and foreigners to the covenants of the promise, without hope and without God in the world. But now in Christ Jesus you who once were far away have been brought near through the blood of Christ. (Ephesians 2:12-13)

FORGIVEN

The woman lies in the dirt
Covered with shame
Clothes hastily pulled on
When her accuser roughly jerked her from the tent
Half naked, the wild look of one held captive
Desperate to be free of her captivity
Jesus looks at her
And really sees her
Not the tousled hair, the eyes full of anger and tears
Not the torn clothes or the shame
He sees her
One who wants to love but has never known love
One who wants to be free of her sin
But knows no other path
One who knows she will probably die for her sins
But is desperate to find one glimpse of grace
And then He writes
"You are forgiven.
You are loved.
You are beautiful.
You are precious.
You are clean.
You are free!"
Grace, written in the dust at the sinners feet

Grace, imprinted upon the heart
Of one worthy of stoning
Grace, imparted to me!
Oh to grace how great a debtor daily I'm constrained
To be

"Then neither do I condemn you," Jesus declared. "Go now and leave your life of sin." (John 8:11)

CHOOSE LIFE

Choose Life
That you may live…
Not etching out an existence
Or escaping in a cloud of smoke
But breathing in every joy
Breathing out every pain
No more stupors
Or cotton candy thoughts
Grasping reality
The good and the bad of it
Tackling it; wrestling it
Living it
And overcoming in the victory
Of your strength
In Christ
One day at a time

The thief comes only to steal and kill and destroy; I have come that they may have life, and have it to the full. (John 10:10)

THE ELDER SISTER

My Father says to me:
Daughter, you have been with me all the time
Working hard and diligently
I know how you have loved me
And how you love me
Everything that is mine is yours
Let me throw you a party today

I party in your Presence today
Rejoicing that my heavenly Father
Gives more than I could ever
Ask or think
I want all that You have for me
Precious Father

Luke 15:11-32

PRAYER FOR MY CHILDREN

The tears spill from my eyes
My heart's on fire
With the desire for my children to know You
I watch their floundering attempts to discover
What the world has to offer
And my heart fills with fear
"God, won't You bring them to Yourself
Let them see You in all Your fullness and glory
So that what they see with their eyes
Will only be the emptiness that it actually is"

As I lay them on the altar
Again
You so plainly speak to me
"Why don't you believe that I love them?"
Gently
You touch the root of my anxiety
The source of my fear
The core of my deepest anguish
So carefully You touch the pain
The sin of my unbelief
You touch me with the sword of Your Spirit

And I can no longer fight
I believe you, Precious Father
Help my unbelief!

He decreed statutes for Jacob and established the law in Israel, which he commanded our forefathers to teach their children, so the next generation would know them, even the children yet to be born, and they in turn would tell their children. Then they would put their trust in God and would not forget his deeds but would keep his commands. (Psalm 78:5-7)

GOD OF ALL

Praise to You, God
The God of the rough and unrefined
The God of the changed drug-addict
The recovering alcoholic
The raspy-voiced chain smoker

Praise and glory to You, Jesus
The God of the refined
The beautiful, the healthy
The polite and sweet

You are the God of all of me
Because I am all those things
Don't ever let me be fooled
By my education or flowing words
Or talents or wisdom
We all stand naked before You
Praise to You, God
Who sees us as we are
And still loves us
"I glory in Your grace"

Therefore, since we have been justified through faith, we have peace with God through our Lord Jesus Christ, through whom we have gained access by faith into this grace in which we now stand. And we rejoice in the hope of the glory of God. (Romans 5:1-2)

SET US FREE

The happy, blissful, blind childhood
Unaware and innocent of evil
Or the power of the evil one in the world
Awakened little by little
To not so nice things
To not so nice people
To beliefs opposed to the God I grew to love
Entangled in a mesh of satanic making
The fetters binding and squeezing
Out all innocence or even hints
Of sweet childhood dreams
That someday wishes could come true

But You come
Powerhouse of love and grace
With Your blood
You burn holes in the net
Until it is dissolved
Tears pool at the bottom of feet
Freshly released from the agony
Of knowing too much
But not enough…
Of You
Gracious, gracious Father

No matter the beginning
You have come to set the sinner free
Praise You God, praise You Father
For Your work in me

You will surely forget your trouble, recalling it only as waters gone by. Life will be brighter than noonday, and darkness will become like morning. You will be secure, because there is hope; you will look about you and take your rest in safety. (Job 11:16-18)

BENEATH THE CROSS

The place beneath the cross
The place of healing, restoration
The place where all becomes new again
Paths are set straight again
Aligned with the Master's plan
No matter how crooked the journey has been
No matter the depth of the darkness
One has been dwelling in
The place beneath the cross
Brings a new beginning
A path of glorious light
Filled with the joy of forgiveness

When you were dead in your sins and in the uncircumcision of your sinful nature, God made you alive with Christ. He forgave us all our sins, having canceled the written code, with its regulations, that was against us and that stood opposed to us; he took it away, nailing it to the cross. And having disarmed the powers and authorities, he made a public spectacle of them, triumphing over them by the cross. (Colossians 2:13-15)

FATHER

Always waiting
Arms open wide
For a visit from his child
No matter how old
No matter how smart
Or proud or rich or poor
Or dirty or clean
Daddy waits for his child
With healing in his tears
With comfort in his voice
With forgiveness in his embrace

When earthly fathers
Are no longer here
Or no longer care
God is always waiting
To be everything to us
A father
Should be

"I will be a Father to you, and you will be my sons and daughters, says the Lord Almighty." (2 Corinthians 6:18)

Seasons of Change

Just as sure as the trees will be stripped of their leaves and the ground covered with snow until the spring flowers appear from beneath the ground, so our lives experience the seasons of change. In one stage of life we might look at someone in a different stage and wonder why all the fuss about this or that problem, but then our spring is over and the hot grueling summer begins. We understand more because we are there.

Sometimes our lives are simply busier than others. At other times, there are long periods of waiting for dreams to be fulfilled, but then the excitement runs so strong because the dream is finally becoming a reality. There are times when our brains are sharp and the words come out witty and sublime. At other times, the stress of everyday living is so much with us that thoughts of the sublime are nowhere near the words swimming around in our brains.

I think it's harder for some people to accept the changing seasons of life with grace and anticipation. Fall has always been a somewhat sad time of year for me because of nostalgic, most likely altered memories of the way things were and will never be again. I must admit, it's hard for me to let go of the past.

But I know that whatever the time, and whatever the season, God knows where we are. He knows what we need; what our desires are; what we should learn from the things we are going through. I have learned it is best to stay close to Him in and out of every season of my life.

MY LIFE

My life, O Lord, is not set in stone
The years have brought changes
Your hand, molding, shaping
Making me
Not a statue carved in granite
But a soft sculpture of silk and foam
Only responding to the touch
Of Your hand
Ready to change as Your will
Unfolds in my life

Do not conform any longer to the pattern of this world, but be transformed by the renewing of your mind. Then you will be able to test and approve what God's will is— his good, pleasing and perfect will. (Romans 12:2)

FREE FALL

The leaves fall through the sky
Like birds who have lost control
Coming from their place of safety
Abiding place
Nestled in the branches of the tree
Green with life and energy
They had their season
They do not cry out
"Let me stay here a little longer"
Their colors change into beauty
and then they are removed
Each year, a season ordained
Predetermined in its rightness
The branches stand naked
Against the cold blue sky
Waiting for the coming
Of fresh, new abiding ones

There is a time for everything, and a season for every activity under heaven. (Ecclesiastes 3:1)

CONTROL

Except a grain of wheat dies
It is never more than just a grain of wheat
Still I hold on, Lord
To some semblance of control
In every area of my life...
And other's lives
Where is the reckless abandon
The total freedom
To believe in You
And trust You to bring about
All that concerns me
Am I missing so much of the abundant life
Simply because I
Have to be
In control?

I tell you the truth, unless a kernel of wheat falls to the ground and dies, it remains only a single seed. But if it dies, it produces many seeds. (John 12:24)

A NEW YEAR

Lord, it's a new year
New thoughts, new plans, new friends
A new song
What will the thoughts be, Lord?
I will seek your bright shining glory
More and more of You
What will the plans be, Lord?
I will watch and see where doors open
Or where they close
Whatever You bring, it will be exciting
Because You are a God of hope

Who will the new friend be, Lord?
I know that You promise
To meet all of our needs
I will look for my fellow intercessor
That person who loves You
More than life
My new friend

What will be the new song be, Lord?
I will sing
Repeat choruses of intimate times

We've had before
With new, added verses
Containing fresh insights
Written with eyes that see things
In a different light

For this New Year
I claim the promises that are in You
Always yes
I am expecting
Joy to burst forth
Amidst the crushed petals
To see
Sunlight dancing in the
Dew drops of pain
I believe that
All is made new
In You

See, the former things have taken place, and new things I declare; before they spring into being I announce them to you." (Isaiah 42:9)

BLANK PAGES

The pages of my life
Are NOT already filled
Empty white sheets
Of expectancy

My bold, hard type
Made marks on all the pages
Filled in till the end
As though I had some control
Over the substance of them

As You wipe clean the past, Lord
Do the same with my future
The future I sought to control
And evenly space out
In between mission work and furloughs
No, I give you all my days
Oh writer of my journey
You alone can fill in the empty space
With songs that will last for eternity
I know Your ending for me
Will be beyond
What I ever could have imagined

My frame was not hidden from you when I was made in the secret place. When I was woven together in the depths of the earth, your eyes saw my unformed body. All the days ordained for me were written in your book before one of them came to be. How precious to me are your thoughts, O God! How vast is the sum of them! (Psalm 139:15-17)

THE GARDENIA

(Written the first year after we moved to Japan)

In this place so far away...
From friends, family
And familiar places
I smell your sweetness
And memories come
Flooding my soul
Bathing me with fresh goodness
Memories of a house long ago
It seems, and yet not so long
A little girl playing hide and seek
With adoring, tolerant sisters

A slightly bigger girl helping
Daddy bring in loads of sweet melons
All sizes
Bushels of succulent summer corn
Cantaloupes which filled the
House and car with their aroma

A younger woman
Aglow with the warmth of first love
Exchanging kisses with her honey
Surrounded by your smell

In this place so far away...
I drink in your fragrance
As the dry ground drinks in
The wetness of the first spring rain
God has sent you to me
To let me taste and see that
He is good
He is here-everywhere with me
Just as your aroma
Engulfs my weary and parched life
His Spirit gently says
Rest in Me
I love you
Thank you, my flower for bringing
To me memories
Memories, which lead me to new joys

*Taste and see that the LORD is good; blessed is the man
who takes refuge in him. (Psalm 34:8)*

HIDDEN BEAUTY

The well runs deep with love and longing
A pool of relentless, restless energy
The calm surface
Hiding depths of determination
Endless supplies of strength and courage
Plethora of pain

I look in the well
And see not the depth
Only a reflection of my own image
But when the wind sends ripples upon the surface
And the murkiness parts for an instant
I discover in the deep waters
Nuggets of pure gold
Righteous beauty tried by fire
Waiting to be discovered
I see crimson rubies
Blood red with compassion and love
Forged in a sensitive heart
I see diamonds not yet ready to be revealed to the world

"The LORD does not look at the things man looks at. Man looks at the outward appearance, but the LORD looks at the heart." (1 Samuel 16: 7b)

GROWING OLD

Keep my eyes clear, Lord
My spiritual sight focused on You
The bright Morning Star
My visual sight unclouded
Even though tired

Keep my mind clear, Lord
Filled with Your word
Letters coming together into
Words and sentences that make sense
Let all the synapses of my brain
Make contact in the right places
So I may fully listen to
And comprehend those around me

Do not let me be bound
By the limitations of this body
No excuses like the disciples
"the spirit is willing but the flesh is weak"
I CLAIM Your resurrection power
Jesus, You healed people all day
And still had compassion

Oh how I want to be like You
Especially this week
With so many opportunities to minister

Let Your light shine through me
Let Your Holy Spirit cover me
So no off-hand comment
Will affect the peace You have given me
I am yours today Lord
Tired or not

Even to your old age and gray hairs I am he, I am he who will sustain you. I have made you and I will carry you; I will sustain you and I will rescue you. (Isaiah 46:4)

ROOTS

Images of narrow streets
With gray slate tile gates and roofs
Pagodas and tori
Sushi bars and ramen shops
Bring up a world of memories
Another world
A different time and place
Where I lost my heart
To a people so far from me
Will the sadness never leave?
The feeling that part of me is gone?
Could I not feel that part of me was gained?
When I grew from a girl to a woman
In my Japan?
The lessons learned in that journey
Cannot be taken from me
The passion for the Japanese to know Jesus
Will not be stifled
Even underneath the heavy burdens
Of church work in the US
I may be there no longer
But it is a part of me
Just as sure as the roots
Grew deep under the willow tree

At our house in Mikage
The roots You grew for me in Japan
Will never die

If I rise on the wings of the dawn, if I settle on the far side of the sea, even there your hand will guide me, your right hand will hold me fast. (Psalm 139:9-10)

JAPANESE SONG OF MEMORIES

The song of the semis (cicadas)
Echoes the cries of my heart
A relentless melody
Pulsing as strong as a current
Constant, driving, never ending
Yet bringing peace
Riding on the waves of memories
Wrapped up in summer evenings
Past and present
Intertwined and melting together
As the song rolls on

I thank my God every time I remember you.
(Philippians 1:3)

LEAVING

The sparkles of the sun upon the water
Fill my soul with Your beauty
Every single place I look
You have prepared for us to leave
Father, I have been so sad that I have not been needed
But You have known –it is time
How else could I leave this place
Where my heart has been buried
Under the weight of the millions of people
Who do not know You

My dear children, for whom I am again in the pains of childbirth until Christ is formed in you. How I wish I could be with you now. (Galations 4:19-20a)

HOME

I marvel at what You have created
In my heart
The sense of home
I have found here already
From black dungeon
Of bottomless self-pity
To joy unspeakable
Because I am with You
I am somebody
In You!!
No title, no job, no recognition
But beloved in Your sight
It is so good to be Your child
I am forever amazed
At Your amazing grace!

Even the sparrow has found a home, and the swallow a nest for herself, where she may have her young— a place near your altar, O LORD Almighty, my King and my God. Blessed are those who dwell in your house; they are ever praising you. Selah (Psalm 84:3-4)

WINTER

Behind the line of naked trees
Lies a field of snow
Pure white beauty
Graceful softness
The slumbering ground underneath
Waits to see what it will become
A field of grain to feed the hungry?
A neighborhood to house the homeless?
Nothing to do now but lie still
Under this blanket of cold beauty
And wait

Wait for the LORD; be strong and take heart and wait for
the LORD. (Psalm 27:14)

A NEW SONG

You have put a new song in my heart
Not the exuberant upbeat song of my youth
Not the confident strong melody of young adulthood
No, the strains of this song
Are deep
Many minor chords fingered in pain
The beat is not my own
But is the heartbeat of the Father
The melody is beautiful, but haunting
Tender but not fragile
My song is rich in harmony
Layered in truth and desire
There is no part of me that does not sing it
It is Jesus!

He put a new song in my mouth, a hymn of praise to our God. Many will see and fear and put their trust in the LORD. (Psalm 40:3)

CONTENTMENT IN THE EMPTY NEST

Let this moment last, Lord
All the ducks in a row
Sun shining, cool crisp air
Each child safely happy
In their own place
Just the two of us
(Three, counting You)
Enjoying a getaway weekend
How blessed I feel
To be happy again
The light is finding me...
At the end of the tunnel

He brought me out into a spacious place; he rescued me
because he delighted in me. (Psalm 18:19)

MY CENTER

The world is spinning fast
Changing from moment to moment
From bad to worse
And I fear, sometimes
That I have lost my center
Things I cannot understand
Complicated, confused, and confounded
Until I find my center again
In You
In You, the world stops spinning
The comfort of sameness prevails
The whirl of satan's offensive attack
Becomes stilled, quelled
And I am liberated
To enjoy the greatest simplicity
Soundness of mind and heart
You are indeed my constant
How I love You, Jesus

Since, then, you have been raised with Christ, set your hearts on things above, where Christ is seated at the right hand of God. Set your minds on things above, not on earthly things. For you died, and your life is now hidden with Christ in God. (Colossians 3:1-3)

MY FATHER

Old man, looking out of vacant eyes
What's behind the garbled speech
The intricate connections of memories
That are no longer connected in the right places
Where is the strength that was my Daddy?
The wisdom he brought to every query
His face flushed; white tufts of hair
In disarray, mind grasping
To sustain a single thought
He is precious to me, my Father
And I know he is precious in your eyes
A treasured gem eighty three years in the making
Certainly not perfect yet
But one day he will be
Stronger than before
And soon, he will see You
And be like You
Wiser than before
Perfect, like the daddy I have always known him to be

And we, who with unveiled faces all reflect the Lord's glory, are being transformed into his likeness with ever-increasing glory, which comes from the Lord, who is the Spirit. (2 Corinthians 3:18)

HYMNS AT A NURSING HOME

Together we sing the good old hymns
As I play them on the piano
"Sweet hour of Prayer"
"Amazing grace"
"The Old Rugged Cross"
When a soft voice comes from beside the piano
"Can we sing, 'I Need Thee Every Hour'?"
His frail lips barely able to form the words
His thin body confined to the wheel chair
Crying out the words, "I need thee, oh, I need thee!!"
My heart and soul sing
As the notes flow from my fingertips

Tears come to my eyes as I hear the fragile
Yet strong voices behind me
We stop the singing and prepare to go to lunch
He grabs my hand and looks deep into my eyes
"You know Him don't you?"
His eyes set in his dark face
Pools of knowledge
A kindred spirit
Someday we will meet again…
In Glory!

However, as it is written: "No eye has seen, no ear has heard, no mind has conceived what God has prepared for those who love him." (1 Corinthians 2:9)

223

HOME GOING

A certain sadness
The prevailing mood
Though laughter
Echoes in the halls
And days long past
Are remembered

Time shared
And new memories made
But always aware
That something has changed...
Is changing

For his anger lasts only a moment, but his favor lasts a lifetime; weeping may remain for a night, but rejoicing comes in the morning. (Psalm 30:5)

IN HEAVEN

In heaven today the angels are singing
With wings outspread
And glorious halos on each head
In heaven today the saints are singing
With heads and hands held high
And voices clear
Daddy is singing
All the words of the songs he loved
In perfect harmony with thousands around him

His mind is clear, not just seeing through a glass, dimly
But face to face
The light of God's glory filling his every thought
His legs are strong, no more pain
The energy and power of the Holy Spirit
Reviving him
Allowing him to run upon the mountains
Not hampered by any form of sinful flesh
His heart is light and filled with love and joy
For he is in the Presence of Joy and Love itself
God Almighty
There is no sadness in his eyes
No tears are waiting to escape

He walks in white raiment
No worries of dirtying it from
Food dropped by a trembling hand
He is thoroughly clean
His heart is pure
He is fully redeemed
Wholly sanctified
Standing without shame
Before the King of Kings
Speechless, perhaps in awe and wonder
Bowing perhaps, in the presence of such majesty
Dancing perhaps, with the joy
Of comprehending the incomprehensible
Knowing even as he is known
Oh, God, You have set my heart in a wide place
You have filled my cup with joy
How I look forward to the day
When all of me is completely Yours

Now we know that if the earthly tent we live in is destroyed, we have a building from God, an eternal house in heaven, not built by human hands. Meanwhile we groan, longing to be clothed with our heavenly dwelling, because when we are clothed, we will not be found naked. For while we are in this tent, we groan and are burdened, because we do not wish to be unclothed but to be clothed with our heavenly dwelling, so that what is mortal may be swallowed up by life. (2 Corinthians 5:1-4)

Joy

Joy is a complex word made simple by an acronym: Jesus, Others, You. But we all know that joy is not found in any seemingly effortless formula. Joy is often elusive and, to many people, unattainable.

Through various tests and trials, I have learned that joy is not at all what I first thought it was. It is not synonymous with the fleeting happiness of a first kiss or a ride on a roller coaster.

It is a peace that passes understanding and is attained when our minds and hearts cease to try and grasp that understanding. It is taking in all that God has to offer in this world, while our souls live in another one. It is found beyond circumstances, beyond human emotion, beyond the realm where satan rules. That's why true joy can never be taken away or altered. It is found only in Him and He is unchangeable.

FILLED TO OVERFLOWING

Filled with peace, not just a fleeting hint of some
Feeling from childhood innocence
But **peace, real peace**
Even in the midst of turmoil
In spite of nasty blocks stacked up to make me fall
Filled with Peace
Filled, full, abundant
Trusting in Him
I am filled
Trusting enough to open wide
No folded arms, no shut mouth, no sewn up heart
Stitched with the needle and thread of past hurts
Kept secrets, oozing still with bitterness
My heart is open, ready to believe again
Receive again, trust again

Trusting in Him
No one else but Jesus
So that I may OVERFLOW with hope
Overflow! Not just filled, full, abundant
But overflowing with hope
Wow!
Hope that keeps me going
Sustains, supports, lifts me up

Hope, by the power of the Holy Spirit
Living in me!
Joy, Peace, Hope
All mine, by the power of the Holy Spirit
Living in me!
Amen!

You have made known to me the path of life; you will fill me with joy in your presence, with eternal pleasures at your right hand. (Psalm 16:11)

May the God of hope fill you with all joy and peace as you trust in him, so that you may overflow with hope by the power of the Holy Spirit. (Romans 15:13)

LIFE IN YOU

My life in You, Holy One
So amazing
Life beyond seeing
Beyond knowing
Beyond breathing
Life, given to me
In abundance of joy
Peace surrounding me
Swimming in and out
Of the holes drilled in me
By suffering
You are here and I behold Your glory

Now to him who is able to do immeasurably more than all we ask or imagine, according to his power that is at work within us, to him be glory in the church and in Christ Jesus throughout all generations, for ever and ever! Amen. (Ephesians 3:20-21)

EASTER

Sunrise of bright colors
Splashes of joy painted on hearts
As delicate as eggs
Broken again and again
To bring forth new life

I pray that the eyes of your heart may be enlightened in order that you may know the hope to which He has called you, the riches of His glorious inheritance in the saints, and His incomparably great power for us who believe. That power is like the working of His mighty strength, which He exerted in Christ when He raised Him from the dead and seated Him at His right hand in the heavenly realms. (Ephesians 1:18-20)

JOY BUBBLES

Today, joy bubbles in my heart
From the place where tears are formed
The spring of life
Covering the good times and bad times
The spring, ever cleansing
In the pain and in the joy
One and the same
To make joy in my suffering
And to know sorrow in my happiness
Not bad and good
All good in You!

You turned my wailing into dancing; you removed my sackcloth and clothed me with joy, that my heart may sing to you and not be silent. O LORD my God, I will give you thanks forever. (Psalm 30:11-12)

SONG OF JOY

Birth a song of joy in my heart today
Giver of new songs
A song of praise
As I gaze into Your loveliness
The Morning's glory
You are the color in my day
The writer of my heart's poems
In You alone is my reward

*Those living far away fear your wonders; where morning
dawns and evening fades you call forth songs of joy. You
care for the land and water it; you enrich it abundantly. The
streams of God are filled with water to provide the people
with grain, for so you have ordained it. (Psalm 65:8-9)*

THE DANCE

Two steps forward and one step back
Round and round and round we go
The dance of life
Learning it is half the fun
Rejoicing as I go
The pattern patiently placed
At our feet by the Father's hand
How carefully He orchestrates my mistakes
Into His pattern
In order for the final performance
To be as beautiful
As He always pictured it

Then I heard what sounded like a great multitude, like the roar of rushing waters and like loud peals of thunder, shouting: "Hallelujah! For our Lord God Almighty reigns. Let us rejoice and be glad and give him glory! For the wedding of the Lamb has come, and his bride has made herself ready. (Revelation 19:6-7)

MARRIAGE

Two dancing together
In unity
Heads held high
In beautiful harmony of body and spirit
Gracefully praising their Father
Their King
"And we cry Holy, Holy, Holy"
He leads, but does not overpower
She dances with all her heart
But takes nothing away
From the strength of his moves
Hands clasped
they circle and circle
Filled with the Spirit
Filled with Love
Filled with Power
The Father sees and is pleased with their joy

When we married
It was three
Not two
The bonds holding us together

Stronger than any earthly glue
Love deeper than the ocean
More vast than the sky
Nothing can separate us
From that love
No testing can harden us
No trial can snip those cords
Because we are tied up in Christ
And He is forever

Also, if two lie down together, they will keep warm. But how can one keep warm alone? Though one may be overpowered, two can defend themselves. A cord of three strands is not quickly broken. (Ecclesiates 4:11-12)

MY LIFE'S SONG

Let my life be a melody of Your grace
Notes flowing with steady rhythm
Pauses here and there
Of breathless surprise
Of awe and wonder
While underneath it all
A steady ripple of Your Spirit
Your hand running over
The strings of my heart
The river of love's song
Echoing in the canyons of my pain
Blending in, fitting in perfect harmony
Joy bursting forth in the symphonic
Overture of my life
Amen and Amen
Let it be so, my Lord and orchestrator of my life

Shout for joy to the LORD, all the earth, burst into jubilant song with music; make music to the LORD with the harp, with the harp and the sound of singing, with trumpets and the blast of the ram's horn— shout for joy before the LORD, the King. (Psalm 98:4-6)

THE GIVER

In loving kindness, You give
And give and give
Always the right time
And always the best way

Sometimes our gifts are bargaining tools...
For love, or time, or something in return
But not Yours...
Sometimes our gifts are afterthoughts
"Whoops, I forgot that birthday
What will they think..."
But not Yours...
Each one so carefully laid out
Before the foundation of the world
I will accept all of Your gifts today, O Lord!
The rain as well as the sunshine
The tears and the laughter together
Why does it feel like today is my birthday?

Every good and perfect gift is from above, coming down from the Father of the heavenly lights, who does not change like shifting shadows. (James 1:17)

YOUR FACE

Your face is before me
Holiness glows from Your head
Your eyes shine with the brightness of hope
The deep blue of Your compassion
Melts any resistance to Your embrace
Your mouth speaks words of kindness
And I see the twinkle of Your eyes
As I approach
Running to jump onto Your lap

When I wrap my arms around You
Your whole face lights up with a smile
"How I love you, child I love you!"
With my eyes fixed on Your face
I tell You everything
And Your heart listens to my heart
With an understanding too deep for words
Oh, the joy of being in Your Presence
"I love You, daddy!"

*My heart says of you, "Seek his face!" Your face, LORD, I
will seek. (Psalm 27:8)*

KEEP IN STEP

Keep in step with the Spirit
Joy bouncing in light-hearted freedom
Steady rhythm of strength
Consistently undergirding
Picking me up
And lifting me
Above the clouds
Above the pain
Above the flesh
Winging me to worlds unknown
Dancing with me
In the shadows
Slowly but surely
Bringing me to walk, no, run
In the sunlight
Until one day, I will walk, run, no, soar
With Him in the light of His glorious Son

Do not get drunk on wine, which leads to debauchery.
Instead, be filled with the Spirit. (Ephesians 5:18)

TO KNOW YOU

Sometimes I love You with softness
Like the nudge of a kittens nose
Cuddling up to You
And allowing You to stroke
Places in my heart no one else can touch
Sometimes I love You with steel-like passion
Approaching You with boldness and desire
To know You more
To see Your face
To go so beyond my human limitations
And take hold of You
As You take hold of me

Sometimes I love You with exuberant joy
Dancing in Your Presence
With the abandon of a child
Looking to see the smile on Your face
As your joy is fulfilled in me

No matter how I love You
I will always love You
You are my God, my friend, my Savior
My joy, my passion, my grace, my healer
My encourager
You are everything to me!

I want to know Christ and the power of his resurrection and the fellowship of sharing in his sufferings, becoming like him in his death, and so, somehow, to attain to the resurrection from the dead. (Philippians 3:10-11)

243

A CHOICE

The gnawing feeling in the pit of my stomach
Sadness sending sparks
So many changes in my life
Loneliness hiding in deep crevices
Two choices here
Allow it to gnaw at me all day
Fan the sparks into flame
Ponder on what is past and can be no more
Or come to You
And find joy!!
I did it this morning, Lord
Chose You
And oh, the grace I feel
The joy I know is real
The hope of a day filled
With divine encounters
Awesome God
How quickly You make the path straight
And I am able to walk again

You have made known to me the path of life; you will fill me with joy in your presence, with eternal pleasures at your right hand. (Psalm 16:11)

THE GOSPEL CONCERT (REAL JOY)

(Written after a gospel concert of mostly nonChristians
in Kobe, Japan)

Wisps of dreamlike happiness
Dance upon the choir member's faces
Exuberant joy floats in the air
Arms stretched high, to touch some piece of happiness
Fingers grasp for a moment
The joy that so eludes them
The music stops
The dream is gone
All that remains are the memories of a good time
A CD or tape to remind them that there is joy
somewhere

Oh that they would seek for more
Than a one time good time
The reality of Jesus
The sure, steadfast, solid rock, which brings
Unspeakable, immovable peace
Not elusive happiness, but joy, which bubbles up
From a living well
And breaks forth in song

More than a good feeling
May they seek forgiveness in the fact of the cross
The reality of the blood
The power of the resurrection
And the dream will never end
The song will go on for eternity

For he has rescued us from the dominion of darkness and
brought us into the kingdom of the Son he loves, in whom
we have redemption, the forgiveness of sins.
(Colossians 1:13-14)

God's Voice

How do you describe what you cannot see with your eyes or hear with your ears? Something as real to you as the wind upon your cheek but just as invisible?

God's voice is a whisper in my heart; a thunderous revelation in my spirit. It leaps off the pages of His written word and is given human voice in the sermons I hear or the words of encouragement from family and friends. His words flow through me as I write the poems He gives to me.

I hear His voice in the bird's song or a baby's cry or beautiful music or even the new, sometimes innovative songs by my piano students. When I am listening, He speaks volumes throughout my days.

That's the key: 'when I am listening.' God speaks to everyone, everywhere. Few take the time to stop and listen. Our lives are overcrowded, spiritually undernourished, and most of the time, unavailable to Him. I wonder how many messages I have missed along the way because other sounds were filling my ears.

ONLY YOU

There are no requests
On my lips this morning
Only a desire to hear You
There will be no knocking
This morning
I come to the garden alone
Longing to hear the voice of the angels

Again my heart is stirred
To yearn after revival
A manifestation of Your Presence
So strong that no one could mistake it
Holy Father of glory
Thank you for meeting me here

O God, you are my God, earnestly I seek you; my soul thirsts for you, my body longs for you, in a dry and weary land where there is no water. (Psalm 63:1)

GOD'S VOICE

Engulfed in Your sweet Holy Presence
The world seems far away
The brushing against my skin
Is like the kiss of Your Spirit to my heart
How good it is to be with You

Calmly, slowly, I bend my knees
I give my ear to capture Your voice
Speak to me Jesus
I'm not looking for answers
Only You do I seek
In the finding of You
My questions will be filled

I love those who love me, and those who seek me find me. (Proverbs 8:17)

CREATOR GOD

A million stars in the sky
And You placed each one just so
Their tails spin out of orbit
And You catch them in Your outstretched hand

You look on fields of flowers
And the splendor of their colors
Sing to You in praise
Their crushing becomes perfume in Your courts

You gaze upon the vast ocean
And grin at the playful porpoise
You watch the way Your creation
Masks itself to keep from being eaten

If You hold the stars in Your hands
And the perfume of the crushed in Your nose
If Your eyes contain the fish of the sea
How much more do You esteem
The crown of Your creation

When my light, like a falling star
Begins to go out
You catch me in Your hand
And hold me so gently

When I am filled with the color of joy
My praises give You pleasure
And when I am crushed, the perfume of my sorrow
Is incense before You

When I hide myself in pretense and disguise
To keep from being hurt
I know Your eye is on me
And I cannot hide from You

Oh to know that You treasure me so
That Your hand should cover me, surround me
That You absorb the beauty of my pain
That Your eyes catch everything that concerns me

"How precious are Your thoughts to me, Oh, Lord how great is the sum of the them. If I should count them, they would be more in numbers than the sand." (Psalm 139:17)

251

PRECIOUS TO ME

The sun pouring down over the sky blue bridge
Purple wisteria peeking out
Promising to become an array of splendor
I walk to Friendship House to help someone discover
The beauty of Easter
Singing praises, I make the familiar trek
My heart as light as the cool mountain air
Filled with the joy of being a child of God
I speak to Him
"Lord, it's a pleasure to walk with You today"
A child's exuberance, "I love you, Daddy"
And You answer back
"It's a pleasure to walk with you, too"
Yahweh, the God of Easter
The Creator of Splendor
The Author of the Sun
The Painter of the Flowers
Takes pleasure in walking with me!
I cannot express the joy that fills my soul
As I hear His voice of love
He loves me and takes pleasure in me
May every day be so rich!!

Since you are precious and honored in my sight, and because I love you, I will give men in exchange for you, and people in exchange for your life. (Isaiah 43:4)

INTENSE SOFTNESS

To play the piano
To pour my heart out in song
To give my all to evangelize
To overflow from the well-spring
Of enthusiasm and confidence
To so passionately believe something
That all those around me know it

More is not all the time better
Back off a little, the choir director says
Blend, match your sound, make harmony
Keep the intensity but make it soft
KEEP THE INTENSITY BUT MAKE IT SOFT!
What a loud voice I have been making all these years
Loud in my passion and my enthusiasm
Loud in making my opinions known
Lord, forgive me for not listening
To the subtle tones of Your voice
Forgive me for striving so hard
And not being still enough
Not just in my quiet time
But even when I am passionate about something
Backing off when it's time

Letting my music be the sweet foundation
On which another's glory is built

"Be still, and know that I am God; I will be exalted among the nations, I will be exalted in the earth." *(Psalm 46:10)*

YOUR ARM

Your strong mighty arm reaches out
Glowing, stretching, strong
But gentle
You reach down from heaven
And with palm outstretched
Wait for me to put my hand in Yours

Your voice says," It's time to get up and walk
No more cowering under my wings"
Oh, the softness and power in the voice
The strength in that hand
I will walk and not faint
Run and not be weary
For my Savior's hand upholds me

The eternal God is your refuge, and underneath are the everlasting arms. He will drive out your enemy before you, saying, 'Destroy him!' (Deuteronomy 33:27)

HE SPEAKS

The soft sound of rain
A sky full of black clouds
Dulls the mind sometimes
God doesn't want it that way
He speaks in the wind
I am truth

A night of shattered plans
No one to share with
Lost in a world of unfulfilled dreams
He speaks in my loneliness
I am comfort

Many friends around
But no one who cares
Wanting to be loved and needed
God speaks in my need
I will provide

Nothing going right
Attitudes all wrong
No strength to go on
God speaks in my weakness
I am strong

Lying in bed
Music playing in other rooms
Thinking of you
God speaks in my thoughts
I am love

High spirited nights of ecstasy
Feeling close to you
Being close to God
He speaks in our closeness
I am the perfect bond

Depressed, discouraged
Unhappy
Wanting to give up
Disgusted at futile efforts to be perfect
God speaks in my hopelessness
I am hope

Baby blue sky, studded with fluffy
white clouds
Mountains tall and majestic
Clear strong stream

In our awe God speaks
I AM

Moses said to God, "Suppose I go to the Israelites and
say to them, 'The God of your fathers has sent me to you,'
and they ask me, 'What is his name?' Then what shall I tell
them?" God said to Moses, "I am who I am. This is what
you are to say to the Israelites: 'I AM has sent me to you.'"
(Exodus 3: 13-14)

MY ROCK

I come to the rock that is higher than I
Stronger than I
More constant than I
As I lay myself, a living sacrifice
Upon this stony altar
My soul becomes as You are
Strength comes from forgiveness
Confidence comes from my silence
Allowing You to speak to me
Softly to me...
Once again smoothing out the jagged edges
Giving me grace to be able to give today
Where once the pot stood empty
Now, it is full of new wine and oil
Giving joy, soothing healing
Lubrication for those things
Which will inevitably rub me wrong today
You are, indeed,
All that I need

I love you, O LORD, my strength. The LORD is my rock, my fortress and my deliverer; my God is my rock, in whom I take refuge. He is my shield and the horn of my salvation, my stronghold. (Psalm 18:1-2)

STREAM

Sitting by the water stream
Watching the clear purity
Running over the rocks
Overcoming trees and debris
In its path
I feel Your presence
The Living Water
Trickling, flowing, gushing
Filling my very soul
Always the same
Running, cleansing
Overcoming me

*Whoever believes in me, as the Scripture has said, streams
of living water will flow from within him." (John 7:38)*

ARE YOUR PLEASED?

How many times have I prayed and prayed and prayed
Until I heard what I wanted to hear
"Go ahead and do it"
My heart was excited
My adventure begun
I didn't stop to check
If what I felt was peace
I didn't quit voicing my plans
Long enough to hear
If You were pleased
Or not

Peter said to Jesus, "Lord, it is good for us to be here. If you wish, I will put up three shelters—one for you, one for Moses and one for Elijah." While he was still speaking, a bright cloud enveloped them, and a voice from the cloud said, "This is my Son, whom I love; with him I am well pleased. Listen to him!" When the disciples heard this, they fell facedown to the ground, terrified. (Matthew 17:4-6)

COLORS

Your voice comes to me sometimes
In shades of gray and blue
Softly whispering among my other thoughts
And I am unclear
About Your path for me

Sometimes Your voice comes to me
Like a bright yellow beam
Penetrating my soul
"This is my will, walk in it"
And I can clearly see
And eagerly obey

Thank you for the colors of Your voice, Lord
Even though I complain
About the blue times
Actually, in the dim light
I am forced to wait
And quieten my heart
Bringing my every thought to You
And I am able to rest in the beauty
Of Your shade

Ascribe to the LORD the glory due his name; worship the LORD in the splendor of his holiness. The voice of the LORD is over the waters; the God of glory thunders, the LORD thunders over the mighty waters. The voice of the LORD is powerful; the voice of the LORD is majestic. (Psalm 29:2-4)

AWAY FROM THE STORM

The sheets of wetness beat against the tiled roof tops
Dancing on the window panes
With a fervor juxtaposed against my calmness

In this room, where You are with me
There is no fog
No gushing wind or rain
Only a still small voice
Engulfing me, keeping me, holding me

I see Your glory in the rain
I perceive Your power in the wind
But in my quiet place
It is Your love that I feel

The LORD said, "Go out and stand on the mountain in the presence of the LORD, for the LORD is about to pass by." Then a great and powerful wind tore the mountains apart and shattered the rocks before the LORD, but the LORD was not in the wind. After the wind there was an earthquake, but the LORD was not in the earthquake. After the earthquake came a fire, but the LORD was not in the fire. And after the fire came a gentle whisper.

When Elijah heard it, he pulled his cloak over his face and went out and stood at the mouth of the cave. Then a voice said to him, "What are you doing here, Elijah?"
(1 Kings 19:11-13)

THE STRENGTH OF YOUR VOICE

The thunder rolls
Shaking the very foundation
Of earth and human frames
Reeling the strength of the ages
Across the lightening lit sky
Awesome power displayed
Disrupting dreams in the night

Your words thunder in my mind
Shaking the foundation of my thoughts
Those thoughts from my human weakness
Fall and crumble
While Your word in my heart
Remains strong
Your love pierces my darkness
Shattering barricades set up by satan
To make me feel empty, unloved
I bow at the sound of Your voice
My heart responds to Your wooing
I've come to You this midnight
Speak to me, O Lord

(Jesus said): Father, glorify your name!" Then a voice came from heaven, "I have glorified it, and will glorify it again. "The crowd that was there and heard it said it had thundered; others said an angel had spoken to him. Jesus said, "This voice was for your benefit, not mine.
(John 12:28-30)

YOU ARE HERE

The bird's sing in the trees behind me
Loud and distinctive
Soft and fluttering
The cool breeze caresses my face
I lift my eyes to the sunshine
And I know You are here
You are here in this beauty
In my heart
You are here

For since the creation of the world God's invisible qualities—his eternal power and divine nature—have been clearly seen, being understood from what has been made, so that men are without excuse. (Romans 1:20)

WHOLLY SATISFIED

I am wholly satisfied, Lord
You ARE good
And Your mercies endure forever
You lead me through the places
Where I doubt Your very goodness
You speak to me
Even when my head is down
But when you lift my head
To see You
My cup runneth over

You prepare a table before me in the presence of my enemies. You anoint my head with oil; my cup overflows. (Psalm 23:5)

THE WAY YOU LOOK AT ME

The moon stares at me from its spot way above the trees
The rays extending to the deepest parts of me
The crescent, not yet full, sees all
Like a diamond in its beauty
Pure
Pure white, shining bright with knowing

I felt Your Presence this early morning, Lord
Your eye is upon my family and me
I feel Your protection, Your grace
I am comforted by Your gaze

Your thoughts of me are pooled together
To make the widest and brightest star
I am overwhelmed by your love
I sit in Your Presence, unafraid
There is nothing to hide
Nothing that can be hidden
It's taken a long time
To find this place

How precious to me are your thoughts, O God! How vast is the sum of them! Were I to count them, they would outnumber the grains of sand. When I awake, I am still with you. (Psalm 139:17-18)

JESUS, THE I AM

You come to me
Lost, broken, torn
And I hold you in my arms
Feel the warmth of Me
The love in Me
You will hear my soothing voice
Call your name
For you are my sheep
And I am your Shepherd

You come to Me,
Hungry
The things of this world
Not satisfying your soul
Come to Me
You who are heavy laden
And I will give you rest
My arms are open wide
My light beckons you
You are drawn to my brightness
My spirit shouts
As you dance before me in joy
Dancing in my strength
Rejoicing in my safety

I am pleased to be
The light of your world

You come to me
And lay yourself on the altar
As I have asked
I know your dreams have died
Your ambitions are gone
Your strength has failed
I know what you have given for me
When I was on your earth
I had dreams
Of all the good I could do
All the people I could heal
All the demons I would cast out
In my fleshly body
I had desires
But I gave my life for you
I laid it all down
And died
For you
It was worth it
The victory came
The victory is here for you

I AM the resurrection and the Life
She who believes in me
Though she dies, will live again

Come to me
And I will show you
The treasures of heaven
Grace abounding
The richest of colors
The sounds of the angels
Come to me
Out of your blindness
Out of you darkness
And I will open up to you
The glory of all ages
Come to Me
And I will show you who
I AM

When Jesus spoke again to the people, he said, "I am the light of the world. Whoever follows me will never walk in darkness, but will have the light of life." (John 8:12) "I tell you the truth," Jesus answered, "before Abraham was born, I am!" (John 8:58) "I am the good shepherd. The good shepherd lays down his life for the sheep. (John 10:11) Jesus said to her, "I am the resurrection and the life. He who believes in me will live, even though he dies. (John 11-25)

GRACE TO YOU

Grace… to live a life unfettered
By feelings of inadequacy
Grace… to believe in yourself
As God believes in you
Grace… to laugh in the face of obstacles
To love in spite of...
Grace… to the downtrodden and discouraged
To the praise-filled and joy-driven

His grace be unto you

Glimpses Into the Life of the Author

When I was thirteen, I gave my whole life to God: to go anywhere He desired, to do anything He wanted of me, and to be all that He desired me to be. He led me to marry my wonderful (and patient) husband, Michael, who also desired to go anywhere God would lead. After we both graduated from New Orleans Baptist Seminary, we took our first son, Phillip, and moved to the inner city of Baltimore, Maryland. As home missionaries, we learned to live and minister in a culture different than our hometown of Atlanta, Georgia.

It wasn't long before God lay on our hearts the call to go to Japan as foreign missionaries. Filled with fear of the unknown and sadness at leaving family, but faith in the God who called us, we embraced the adventure. Taking our two boys (Andrew was born in Baltimore), we began learning yet another far different culture and language. It was there that God put us through the fire and caused me often to question how difficult it was going to be to become all that He wanted of me.

In our 18 years in Japan we studied the language three years, moved four times, brought our baby girl, Alicia, back with us after furlough, and were privileged to see many enter the kingdom. Our hearts were broken over the ninety-eight percent of Japanese who do not know Jesus.

In our city of Kobe, we experienced the Great Hanshin earthquake, where 6500 died. It was an experience we will never forget. In that same year, a fire at a lake cabin next to the one in which we had been vacationing in, took the life of our daughter's new little friend. Through all of this suffering, we were discovering much more about the depth of God's comfort and love.

God continued shaping us during the next years of trials. He was speaking, assuring us of His Presence. He led us back to America, which was a much harder adjustment than I had ever anticipated.

God is now allowing us to see His heart for the poor as we work in the inner city of Columbus, Ohio. He is showing me yet another culture and revealing to me the depth of the love He has for all people.

APPENDIX

LaVergne, TN USA
08 January 2011
211666LV00002B/3/P

9 780977 933471